Early American Poets

EARLY AMERICAN POETS

Selected, with an Introduction

by

LOUIS UNTERMEYER

LIBRARY PUBLISHERS

New York

Printed in the United States of America

INTRODUCTION

Amerı́ca did not declare independence in poetry as quickly
or dramatically as in politics. It adhered to many and widely
contrasting traditions before it freed itself from inherited customs, codes, and cultures; it expressed itself through scores of
imitators before it found its own characteristic way of thinking,
reacting, and writing. Throughout the so-called Colonial period,
scenes and situations of the new world were rendered in the
idiom of the old. Forgotten by all but the literary historians,
such versifiers as George Sandys, Thomas Shephard, Anthony
Somerby, Samuel Sewall, William Wood, John Norton, John
Rogers, Richard Steere, Urian Oakes, John Fiske, the more
accomplished Thomas Dudley, John Saffin, Benjamin Thompson, John Seccomb, Thomas Tillam, and even the far more
gifted Edward Taylor, wrote either in the baroque manner
favored by the seventeenth century or the pseudo-classical style
affected by the followers of Du Bartas and Dryden. This is not
surprising. Many of the earliest New England poets were born
in old England; others, born on this side of the Atlantic, were
contemporaries of that belated Elizabethan, Ben Jonson, the
metaphysical John Donne, and John Fletcher, assumed to be
one of Shakespeare's collaborators.

Much of the early poetry—salient exhibits of which are contained in Harold S. Jantz's *The First Century of New England
Verse*—is in the form of occasional rhymes, learned discourses
and lugubrious elegies, elaborate acrostics and tortured "con-
trapuntal" anagrams. Ingenuity took the place of invention.
Many of the rhythmical designs were dexterous but, though
they are remarkable, they are unreadable.

The first American poet of undoubted importance was a

woman, Anne Bradstreet, daughter of Governor Thomas Dudley, himself a poet. Her anonymous volume, published in 1650, was presented with a title which filled the title-page; it began: "The Tenth Muse, Lately Sprung Up in America; or, Several Poems, Compiled with Great Variety of Wit and Learning, full of Delight: Wherein especially is contained a complete Discourse and Description of the Four Elements, Constitutions, Ages of Man, Seasons of the Year, together with an exact Epitome of the Four Monarchies, viz., the Assyrian, Persian, Grecian, Roman. . . ." Much of the work is strained, stuffed with towering baroque images, grotesque antitheses and contorted "Gongorisms." But the promised "Wit and Learning" is undoubtedly there. Moreover, in the midst of her overdecorated "quaternions," those formidable four-part poems, and especially in "Contemplations," a grace, a whimsicality, and what must have been her personal charm come through, while something like nobility is sounded in her valedictory, "Longing for Heaven." The domestic note is not intrusive; it is heard in a volume, modest and winning, published in 1658:

> I had eight birds hatch'd in the nest,
> Four cocks there were, and hens the rest;
> I nurst them up with pain and care,
> Nor cost nor labor did I spare,
> Till at the last they felt their wing,
> Mounted the trees and learned to sing.

Dozens of competent and sometimes interesting poetasters preceded and followed Anne Bradstreet; but it is not until we reach Edward Taylor that we encounter the first American poet to write with almost overwhelming emotion. Unknown until three hundred years after the poet's birth in about 1642, Taylor's work remained buried until a scholar and teacher, Thomas H. Johnson, unearthed and published it. In 1937, engaged in Colonial research, Johnson came upon a passage which revealed that Edward Taylor was the grandfather of Ezra Stiles, an early president of Yale, and that Stiles had deposited the Taylor manuscripts—including more than 300 poems—in the university's library. Johnson deciphered the verses and had some of them printed in the *New England Quarterly*; two years later he issued a volume, far more comprehensive in scope, *The Poetical Works of Edward Taylor*. Johnson maintained that Taylor's writings, and especially the rhapsodic series, "God's Determinations," is "certainly the finest extensive poetic achievement in America before the nineteenth century." Critics were inclined to agree. "The passionate intensity" (continued Johnson, referring particularly to the two-stanza poem "Upon the Sweeping Flood") "may have no counterpart in any Puritan literature, either in England or America; and the tortuous language, reflecting the violence of the mood, underlines Taylor's emotional as well as poetic kinship with Crashaw and Donne." Taylor also indulged in topical and acrostic verses, as ingenious as they were elaborate. "The machinery of puns, quibbles, and poetic conceits intrigued the seventeenth century mind generally, and Taylor is a belated representative of a fashion nearly outmoded." (One of Taylor's alphabetical oddities is reproduced on page 31 as an example of his ability to mix typographical trickery and genuine sentiment.) As a rule, however, Taylor's sentiments rose rapidly into passions. Ecstasy was as much his element as it was Herbert's, Donne's, and Crashaw's. His inspired eccentricities raise religious abstractions into radiance. "His means of achieving this materialization," wrote Harold S. Jantz in *The First Century of New England Verse*, "is his rich store of images drawn from every phase of daily and Sunday life; he rather prefers than scorns to use the homely or plebeian image to embody the most exalted idea, and will even use an occasional vulgarism if it suits his purpose. He may thus be said to domesticate these ideas, to make them familiar and comfortable furnishings for a New England country parsonage."

The communication of familiar and comfortable ideas was

almost as much a part of Colonial literature as the teaching of theology. Puritan literature is by no means as unremittingly grim and austere as it is often pictured. The early verse is enlivened with obviously authentic glimpses of a domestic and far from dour New England. The food and drink, manners and social customs, even the dances and occasional festivities are graphically recorded in the anonymous "Forefathers' Song," a combination of frank folk ballad and high-hearted humor, in the tart couplets of Benjamin Thompson, bemoaning the passing of "the good old days," in Joel Barlow's gustatory pleasures in "Hasty Pudding," John Seccomb's gay inventory catalogued in his "Will," and Royall Tyler's briskly animated rhymes depicting the way Independence Day was observed a century and a half ago.

In the South at least one notable poem, "Bacon's Epitaph, Made by his Man," was composed in the late seventeenth century. Couched in the classically allusive style of the day, it was in the best sense an "occasional" poem and the occasion was the death of a patriot. When Charles II was restored to the throne in 1660, Sir William Berkeley was reinstated as Governor of the Old Dominion of Virginia. As profligate as his master and even more inefficient as a ruler, Berkeley overtaxed the people, denied them justice, and put down all liberals. He fought liberty, education and enlightenment. "Thank God," he once said, "there are no free schools nor printing presses, for learning has brought disobedience and heresy into the world." The exploited and exasperated Colonists looked for a leader to oppose Berkeley; they found one in Nathaniel Bacon, a wealthy planter. In April, 1676, Berkeley placarded Bacon as a rebel and put a price on his head. Civil war seemed imminent. In October Bacon was seized with a mysterious illness—poison was suspected—and he died a few days later. His death brought forth a mass of protesting literature, most of it circulated secretly. Perhaps the most popular piece was the Epitaph—part elegy, part eulogy—supposedly written by Bacon's servant, his "man." It is obvious, however, that the writer was no lackey but Bacon's friend and political adherent, his "man" in the fullest sense of the word.

With Philip Freneau (1752-1832) the background shifted briefly from New England to New Jersey. The change was one in temperament as well as scene. Unlike most of the Colonial authors, Freneau was a soldier, a satirist, an impulsive adventurer and a fervid controversialist. His best poems, however, dispense with wrath and rhetoric and tune themselves to quiet lyricism. A sensitive observer, Freneau was not satisfied to re-state platitudes to abstract Nature; he wrote, with loving exactness, about such native fauna and flora as the whippoorwill, the honey-bee, the katydid, the pumpkin, the common cinquefoil, the wild honeysuckle, and the red-streaked apple. His contemporaries appreciated not only his use of regional material but Freneau's felicities of phrase. Walter Scott admired the American—he knew many of Freneau's poems by heart—and he was not above incorporating a fine figure from Freneau's "To the Memory of the Brave Americans" in the third canto of his "Marmion."

The native note was further emphasized by William Cullen Bryant (1794-1878), often called "the father of American poetry." Influenced at first by Pope, Kirk White, and the "Graveyard School," and later by Wordsworth, Bryant achieved a straightforward simplicity which set him apart from his contemporaries. It is true that his feelings are often too well-controlled, and that his serenity sometimes congeals into frigidity. In "A Fable for Critics" Lowell stated the case against him in the following couplets:

> There is Bryant, as quiet, as cool, and as dignified
> As a smooth, silent iceberg that never is ignified. . . .
> He may rank (Griswold says so) first bard of the nation,
> There's no doubt that he stands in supreme ice-olation.

Nevertheless, Bryant's lines communicate the spirit of the scene. The best of his poems, from the early "Thanatopsis," written at seventeen, to such constantly quoted apostrophes as "To a Waterfowl" and "To the Fringed Gentian," are rich with country sights and smells, the sense of deeply shadowed woods, the passing of brightly plumaged birds, and the love of country which filled him as a quietly proud American. If his poems lack exaltation as well as excitement, they do not fail to assure the reader with their calm affirmation.

With Emerson, Whittier, and Longfellow, the seeds of American poetry, planted, cultivated, and nourished in New England soil, came into full flower. The thinking of the period was powerfully influenced by the utterances of the three poets; their differences as well as their direct impact did much to shape the cultural patterns of their century. Emerson was not only the visionary and revitalizing philosopher, but the stubbornly nonconforming questioner; Whittier was the militant Puritan; Longfellow became the glorifier of simple song.

Emerson, "the God-intoxicated Yankee," placed vision and personal revelation above ritual; he resigned from his pulpit because he believed that true communion was greater than the communion rite. A Transcendentalist in an age of rapidly growing commercialism, Emerson preached the daily application of moral values rather than material standards. "The mind," he insisted, "is the only reality . . . Perhaps the time will come when the sluggard intellect of this continent will look from under its iron lids and fill the postponed expectation of the world with something better than the exertions of mechanical skill."

Emerson's philosophy cannot be tied to a school or reduced to a system. His mind was intuitive and radiated "life, transition, expansion, the spirit in full energy." Flourishing in spontaneous initiative, he declared "Nothing great was ever achieved without enthusiasm." He generated compact and sometimes explosive wisdom in such epigrams as: "An institution is the lengthened shadow of one man". . . . "Wherever a man comes, there comes revolution. The old is for slaves". . . . "Everything great and excellent in the world is in minorities. To be great is to be misunderstood". . . . "The whole of nature is a metaphor of the human mind." As a poet Emerson is often more rewarding to the mind than the ear. Sacrificing music to meaning, he is lyrical by fits and starts; even his most melodic passages are interspersed with knotty rhythms. Yet he spoke up for a native idiom and indigenous subject-matter long before it became popular to stress "the American way." Anticipating the revolutionary proclamations of Whitman, whom Emerson was the first to discover, Emerson brought "The American Scholar" (1837) to a rebellious climax with: "We have listened too long to the courtly muses of Europe. The spirit of the American free man is suspected to be timid, imitative, tame. Public and private avarice make the air we breathe thick and fat. . . . Not so, brothers and friends—please God, ours shall not be so. We will walk on our own feet; we will work with our own hands; we will speak with our own minds."

Something of this rebelliousness is sensed beneath the seemingly mild contours of Whittier's verse. Whittier's bucolics are obviously placid, but his otherwise quiet voice is deceptive. Whittier was not only a non-conformer, he was an embattled Puritan. Most of the New England poets were descended from ministers, scholars, and members of aristocracy; they themselves were leaders of the literati. Whittier's father was a farmer, and the boy was brought up as a working Quaker, whose brief education was paid for by his earnings as a shoemaker. Practically all his youth was spent on the farm, plowing, planting, and performing the countless country chores. The family was large and hard-working; the household is lovingly but accurately portrayed in "Snow-Bound."

Whittier displayed a courageous and intransigent spirit as

soon as he began to write. His first poems were published in the Newburyport *Free Press*, which had just been founded by the fiery William Lloyd Garrison, who became Whittier's earliest and most important influence. Garrison's fight for the abolition of slavery roused Whittier to a high pitch of protest. He wrote hundreds of insurgent poems and editorials; at his own expense he published a pamphlet, *Justice and Expediency;* he was one of the organizers of the American Anti-Slavery Society. He became editor of the *Pennsylvania Freeman*, consecrated Pennsylvania Hall as a Temple of Liberty, and saw the building destroyed by a reactionary mob. He served as the unofficial but acknowledged laureate of all movements for liberation and civil rights. His impassioned "Ichabod" was wrung from the heart of a deeply disappointed man. The poem was a sad but devastating diatribe by a lover of peace, occasioned by Daniel Webster's support of the Fugitive Slave Law and the appeal of Webster (whom Whittier had always admired) to appease the South. Yet, while he was engaged in necessary polemics, Whittier suspected that his politics were adversely affecting his poetry. With wry resignation he admitted that he had left his bucolic scenes in order to turn

> The crank of an opinion mill,
> Making his rustic reed of song
> A weapon in the war of wrong.

Nevertheless, the verses of Whittier still charm us with their concepts as well as with their incongruities. Whether they are devotional, as some of the best of them are, or descriptive, plainly nostalgic or vividly narrative, insurgent or soothing, they vibrate with the very breath of individuality. The idyllic dreamer was also an idol-breaker, and the evocation of the rural scene is only a part of his power. Whittier wrote his own disarming apologia in a "Proem," which he placed at the head of his collected work. One verse reads:

The rigor of a frozen clime
The harshness of an untaught ear,
    The jarring words of one whose rhyme
    Beat often Labor's hurried time,
On Duty's rugged march through storm and strife, are here.

The stature of Henry Wadsworth Longfellow—by far the most popular poet of his day—has been considerably diminished by time and changing tastes. His present status is indicated by such characterizations as "the household poet," "laureate of the hearth," "model of the humbler bards," and other patronizing phrases. It is true that Longfellow's accomplishment could scarcely measure up to his reputation. His poems were quoted and reprinted everywhere. Twenty-four English publishers issued his work; ten thousand copies of "The Courtship of Miles Standish" were sold in London in a single day; "The Song of Hiawatha" was translated into every modern language as well as Latin. His financial success was complemented by the critics' enthusiastic commendations. With the exception of Poe, whose envy was obvious, Longfellow's colleagues could not praise him enough. Even Walt Whitman, who found Longfellow's excess of verbal melody "almost a sickness," declared that Longfellow was "the sort of counteractant most needed for our materialistic, self-assertive, money-worshipping Anglo-Saxon race, and especially for the present age in America—an age tyrannically regulated with reference to the manufacturer, the merchant, the financier, the politician. . . . I should have to think long if I were asked to name a man who has done more, and in more valuable directions, for America."

Nevertheless, the great bulk of Longfellow has shrunk to a few poems—chiefly the pietistic and sentimental ones—in high school textbooks. It is conceded his gift was that of the unaffected singer, that the mood he evokes is that of twilight, the *Abendlied*, a sadness "which resembles sorrow only as the mist resembles rain." But the concessions fail to recognize that Longfellow rises above his didactic moralizing and gentle jingling. Besides being a natural story-teller, in his quiet way he was something of a pioneer. An ardent traveler who absorbed the spirit of the place, Longfellow transplanted the European heritage and translated the romantic spirit of German, Spanish, and Scandinavian poets into his natural idiom. Yet, although he luxuriated in foreign legends, Longfellow was also a champion of the autochthonous note in American life and letters. Such ballads as "The Skeleton in Armor," such declamations as "The Building of the Ship," and such semi-epics as "Hiawatha," and "Evangeline," as well as the half-heroic, half-humorous narration of "The Courtship of Miles Standish," emphasize indigenous subject-matter and indicate a course followed by the next generation: a growing awareness of the vitality of native material.

Although the New England temperament was commonly described as chill, its language laconic, and its outlook grim, there was another aspect of New England which relished badinage and expressed itself in banter. This lighter side was revealed in high-spirited and often brilliant rhymes by Oliver Wendell Holmes and James Russell Lowell. Holmes was the more searching as well as the more accomplished. His style was pungent and persuasive; frequently it achieved a union of science and fantasy. Everything he wrote was polished. Even such deftly turned verses as "Dorothy Q" and "The Last Leaf" sound serious overtones; their blend of wit and muted pathos suggest a sermon delivered in dance tempo.

More casual than Holmes, Lowell was an even nimbler rhymer than his friend and fellow Cambridgian. His father, like Holmes's, was a minister; like Holmes, also, Lowell was an essayist as well as a poet, and both men were famous for their spontaneous and sometimes critical humor. Lowell made fun of his own impassioned predilections in *A Fable for Critics* when he appraised his failure to reach the heights as a poet:

There is Lowell, who's striving Parnassus to climb
With a whole bale of isms tied together with rhyme;
He might get on alone, 'spite of brambles and boulders,
But he can't with that bundle he has on his shoulders.

One of Lowell's most persistent isms was pacifism. A man of
peace, he fought against war everywhere. In particular he op-
posed America's entry into the Mexican War ("The Present
Crisis"), and the intensity of his anti-war sentiments in "The
Biglow Papers" impressed even the most hot-headed of his
readers. Inventing as his mouthpiece a character named "Birdo-
fredum Sawin"—an outrageous pun with a New England twang
—Lowell satirized the complacency of his times and the hypoc-
risy of the sanctimonious in a vernacular of unsuspected force.
Much of Lowell's work has the fault of the improvising organist
in his Prelude to "The Vision of Sir Launfal"; it begins (and
often continues) "doubtfully and far away." But the uncertain-
ties, the dialect, the trick rhymes and the trivial word-plays, are
finally reconciled by the man's humanity. Using a scholar's
erudition without pretension, the humorist and the idealist are
somehow integrated.

Among the so-called "lesser New England figures" by far the
most interesting are Jones Very, Henry David Thoreau, William Ellery Channing II, and John Godfrey Saxe.

Very's poetry is little known and practically unread, but no
purer verse was written by any of his contemporaries. Emerson,
who spoke glowingly of him in his *Journals*, said that Very had
"an unquestionable stamp of grandeur," and William Ellery
Channing considered him "an oracle of God." Other than
lengthening the last line of the classical sonnet with an extra
foot, Very attempted no innovations; as a firm believer in tradition he worked serenely within the formal pattern. Yet Very's
simple faith surpassed in intensity the rhetoric of the rapt mystic.
In every trivial circumstance—a growing tree, a robin's half-
built nest, the opening of a wind-flower, the coming of day—

Very celebrated universal law; a God-seeker he found God everywhere.

William Ellery Channing II loved the oddities of nature. Unlike Very, who appreciated the simple, Channing seized on the strange and spectacular. For him the earth-spirit bound the caverns of the sea with weedy hair, polished the green ice, gleamed the wall with white frost; his highway was the "unfeatured air" and his consorts were the sleepless stars. With whimsical nonchalance Channing turned the parts of speech upside down and used an accent which was both teasing and tart.

Famous for his prose Henry David Thoreau, that provocative non-conformer, has only recently been recognized as a poet. The roughness of his lines and the frequent obliqueness of his allusions have kept readers from whole-hearted enjoyment of his verse. Yet in his poetry Thoreau sounded the same contradiction of resignation and intransigence, of wryness and tenderness, that distinguished "A Week on the Concord and Merrimack Rivers" and "Walden, or Life in the Woods."

John Godfrey Saxe was the village wonder: the educator and politician turned humorist. A born Vermonter—his birthplace, Saxe's Mills, practically belonged to the family—Saxe spent most of his life in his native state, and no one was more surprised than Saxe himself when the local superintendent of schools became a national celebrity. Forgotten today except for a few anthology pieces, his *Poems*, which went through more than fifty editions in the 1860's, still retain much of the author's homely wisdom and homespun wit.

The group which had its center in Boston and Cambridge dominated American literature from Colonial times to the time of the Civil War. Its eminence was not challenged until the advent of Poe. A few sporadic and, in every sense, occasional writers claimed transitory attention. Joseph Rodman Drake (remembered for "The Culprit Fay," if remembered at all), Fitz-Greene Halleck (author of the declamation piece, "Marco

Bozzaris") Charles Fenno Hoffman, Park Benjamin, Nathaniel
P. Willis, and other members of the New York literati, sometimes called the Knickerbocker School, failed to make more than
an ephemeral impression. The solitary Herman Melville, com-
pletely neglected in his day, was a powerful, unclassifiable
phenomenon.

In the South Edward Coote Pinkney, William Gilmore
Simms, and the rococo Thomas Holley Chivers anticipated the
romantic elegances and, above all, the excesses of Edgar Allan
Poe. At his best Poe fashioned lyrics that were pure music; at
his worst he turned out jingles that were sheer nonsense. A dis-
cerning analyst and shrewd appraiser of other poets' weaknesses,
Poe was a singularly incompetent critic of his own work; he
never learned to separate the genuinely inspired from the obviously third-rate. His poetry, like his prose, is not a fusion but
a disintegrating mixture of baroque fantasies and Gothic gro-
tesques, of horrors framed in sentimentalities, of real roses
inextricably twined about imitation gargoyles.

The key of Poe's maladjustment to life is found in the
dichotomy of his work. Nowhere is it more significantly indicated than in the lines beginning:

> From childhood's hour I have not been
> As others were. I have not seen
> As others saw—I could not bring
> My passions from a common spring—
> From the same source I have not taken
> My sorrow—I could not awaken
> My heart to joy at the same tone—
> And all I loved, I loved alone.

This sense of being removed from the "common spring" of
ordinary joys and sorrows prevented Poe from seeing "as others
saw" and being "as others were." His was, as Longfellow
wrote, "a supersensitive nature chafed by some indefinite sense

xvii

of wrong." Suffering from conscious resentments and unconscious wrongs, Poe became what he imagined himself to be: the "weary, way-worn wanderer," the haunted, self-doomed, always maladjusted outcast. His was the music of another world, a world ruled unconcernedly by angels and demons dedicated to "the viol, the violet, and the vine." In that world of lonely shapes and unearthly shadows the spirit of Poe was unhappily at home.

The year 1819 marked the birth of three authors who reflected three widely differing aspects of the American spirit: James Russell Lowell, Herman Melville, and Walt Whitman. Lowell still upheld the New England tradition in attitude and accent. Melville broke away from the polite tone and polished craftsmanship of the period and, in bursts of violent energy and desperate doubt, created a set of allegories epic in scope and mythical in grandeur. Rebelling against all influences, hurling himself into print with a welter of manifestoes disguised as meditations, Whitman accomplished a one man revolution in form and feeling. With Whitman the early period comes to an end and modern American poetry begins.

Note: Like all anthologies this compilation is self-limiting. Within the limitations, however, it suggests an unusually wide range and varied terrain. The color and climate of a growing country are indicated by the diverse levels of style and subject-matter. In poetry, as in the other arts, the valleys are needed as well as the peaks, and the so-called "popular verse" of the period has a historic value if not always a high esthetic one. If it is objected that patriotic poems are not masterpieces of culture, it can be maintained that the people's poetry is often as true a guide to a nation's development as the choice of the academic critic. This collection is therefore devoted to the expanding spirit as well as the formative genius of America.

Louis Untermeyer.

CONTENTS

INTRODUCTION   v

ANONYMOUS (17th Century)
Forefathers' Song   1

THOMAS DUDLEY (1576-1653)
A New England Gentleman's Epitaph   3

ANNE BRADSTREET (1612-1672)
Contemplations   4
"As Weary Pilgrim"   12

THOMAS TILLAM (1612?-1669?)
Upon The First Sight of New England   14

MICHAEL WIGGLESWORTH (1631-1705)
Vanity of Vanities   15

JOHN SAFFIN (1632-1710)
To Her, Coming Home   20

ANONYMOUS (17th Century)
Bacon's Epitaph, Made by his Man   21

BENJAMIN THOMPSON (1642-1714)
The Good Old Times   23

EDWARD TAYLOR (1642?-1729)
The Ebb and Flow   25
Upon What Base Was Fixed the Lath Wherein   26
Housewifery: I   26
Housewifery: II   27
Upon the Sweeping Flood   28
What Love Is This   28
Oh! What a Thing Is Man   29
This Dove & Olive Branch   31

JOHN SECCOMB (1708-1793)
Father Abbey's Will   32

CONTENTS

FRANCIS HOPKINSON (1737-1791)
The Battle of the Kegs — 36

PHILIP FRENEAU (1752-1832)
From "The House of Night" — 40
The Indian Burying Ground — 41
Song of Thyrsis — 43
On Observing a Large Red-streak Apple — 43
On the Death of Benjamin Franklin — 45
Stanzas — 46
To a Honey Bee — 48

JOEL BARLOW (1754-1812)
Hymn to Peace — 50
The Pudding Praised — 51
The Pudding Prepared — 54
The Pudding Eaten — 57
Freedom — 58

ROYALL TYLER (1757-1826)
Independence Day — 60

JOHN QUINCY ADAMS (1767-1848)
To the Sun-Dial — 62

JOSEPH HOPKINSON (1770-1842)
Hail, Columbia — 63

FRANCIS SCOTT KEY (1779-1843)
The Star-Spangled Banner — 65

SAMUEL WOODWORTH (1785-1842)
The Bucket — 67

JOHN PIERPONT (1785-1866)
Whittling — 69
The Pilgrim Fathers — 70
Warren's Address at Bunker Hill — 72

RICHARD HENRY DANA (1787-1879)
The Little Beach Bird — 74

RICHARD HENRY WILDE (1789-1847)
My Life is Like the Summer Rose — 76

CONTENTS

FITZ-GREENE HALLECK (1790-1867)
On the Death of Joseph Rodman Drake   77

JOHN HOWARD PAYNE (1791-1852)
Home, Sweet Home   79

WILLIAM CULLEN BRYANT (1794-1878)
To a Waterfowl   81
Thanatopsis   82
To the Fringed Gentian   85
The Yellow Violet   86
Song of Marion's Men   87
America   89
The Death of Lincoln   91
From "The Antiquity of Freedom"   92

JOSEPH RODMAN DRAKE (1795-1820)
The American Flag   94

JAMES GATES PERCIVAL (1795-1856)
Seneca Lake   97

GEORGE HILL (1796-1871)
Leila   99

EDWARD COOTE PINKNEY (1802-1828)
Serenade   100
A Health   100

GEORGE POPE MORRIS (1802-1864)
Woodman, Spare That Tree   103

RALPH WALDO EMERSON (1803-1882)
Hymn   105
The Rhodora   106
Forbearance   106
The Snow-Storm   107
Fate   108
Good-bye   108
The Hero   109
Mithridates   110
Two Rivers   111
Wealth   112

CONTENTS

Days   114
The Apology   114
Bacchus   115
Give All to Love   117
Experience   119
Ode   120
Uriel   124
Music   126
Fable   126
History   127
Brahma   128
Terminus   128

HENRY WADSWORTH LONGFELLOW (1807-1882)
The Arsenal at Springfield   131
The Jewish Cemetery at Newport   133
Nature   135
The Building of the Ship   136
The Arrow and the Song   149
A Psalm of Life   150
The Rainy Day   151
Hymn to the Night   152
Milton   153
Chaucer   154
The Village Blacksmith   154
The Tide Rises, the Tide Falls   156
My Lost Youth   157
Snow-Flakes   160
The Skeleton in Armor   161
The Discoverer of the North Cape   167
Sandalphon   171
The Children's Hour   173
Hiawatha's Childhood   175
The Day Is Done   182

JOHN GREENLEAF WHITTIER (1807-1892)
Laus Deo!   185
My Triumph   187

CONTENTS

The Eternal Goodness 190
Ichabod 194
Barbara Frietchie 195
The Waiting 198
The Trailing Arbutus 199
Maud Muller 200
The Barefoot Boy 205
Skipper Ireson's Ride 209
From "Snow-Bound" 212
The Moral Warfare 220

THOMAS HOLLEY CHIVERS (1809-1858)
Apollo 222
Song to Isa Singing 223

EDGAR ALLAN POE (1809-1849)
To Helen 225
A Dream within a Dream 225
Israfel 226
The Haunted Palace 228
The City in the Sea 230
Annabel Lee 232
To One in Paradise 234
Romance 235
To Science 235
The Raven 236
Ulalume 241
To F—— 244
To My Mother 245
For Annie 245
Dream-Land 249
The Sleeper 251
Sonnet: Silence 253
The Lake. To—— 254
The Valley of Unrest 255
Eldorado 256
Alone 257

CONTENTS

OLIVER WENDELL HOLMES (1809-1894)

    The Chambered Nautilus   258
    Old Ironsides   259
    Dorothy Q.   260
    The Last Leaf   263
    The Deacon's Masterpiece   265
    The Ballad of the Oysterman   269
    My Aunt   270
    The Height of the Ridiculous   272
    Unsatisfied   273

ANONYMOUS (1810-1860)

    Seven Negro Spirituals
        My Lord, what a morning   275
        O, by an' by   275
        Steal away   276
        They crucified my Lord   277
        Sometimes I feel like a motherless child   278
        Ezekiel saw the wheel   278
        I got a robe   279

JONES VERY (1813-1880)

    Enoch   281
    The Spirit-Land   281
    The Latter Rain   282
    Nature   282
    Day   283
    The Wind-Flower   284
    Morning   284
    The Tree   285
    October   285
    The Robin   286
    The New World   286
    The Dead   287

JOHN GODFREY SAXE (1816-1887)

    The Blind Men and the Elephant   288
    My Familiar   290
    Early Rising   292

CONTENTS

HENRY DAVID THOREAU (1817-1862)

Independence 295
Smoke 296
Mist 296
Haze 297
All Things Are Current Found 297
Summer Rain 298
Men Say They Know Many Things 300
Love 300
Conscience 301

WILLIAM ELLERY CHANNING, II (1818-1901)

Hymn of the Earth 303
The Earth-Spirit 304
And Here the Hermit Sat 305

JAMES RUSSELL LOWELL (1819-1891)

The Courtin' 306
To a Recruiting Sergeant 310
The Pious Editor's Creed 316
What Mr. Robinson Thinks 320
Prelude to "The Vision of Sir Launfal" 322
Whittier 325
Freedom 327

HERMAN MELVILLE (1819-1891)

Father Mapple's Hymn 329
The Night-March 330
The Maldive Shark 330
Gold in The Mountain 331
The March Into Virginia 331
From "The Martyr" 332
L'Envoi 334

ANONYMOUS

(SEVENTEENTH CENTURY)

Forefathers' Song

New England's annoyances you that would know them,
Pray ponder these verses which briefly doth show them.

The place where we live is a wilderness wood,
Where grass is much wanting that's fruitful and good,
Our mountains and hills and our valleys below,
Being commonly covered with ice and with snow.
And when the north-west wind with violence blows,
Then every man pulls his cap over his nose:
But if any's so hardy and will it withstand,
He forfeits a finger, a foot, or a hand.

But when the Spring opens we then take the hoe,
And make the ground ready to plant and to sow.
Our corn being planted and seed being sown,
The worms destroy much before it is grown;
And when it is growing, some spoil there is made
By birds and by squirrels that pluck up the blade;
And when it is come to full corn in the ear,
It is often destroyed by raccoon and by deer.

And now our garments begin to grow thin,
And wool is much wanted to card and to spin;
If we can get a garment to cover without
Our other in-garments are clout upon clout:

I

Our clothes we brought with us are apt to be torn,
They need to be clouted soon after they're worn,
But clouting our garments they hinder us nothing,
Clouts double are warmer than single whole clothing.

If fresh meat be wanting to fill up our dish,
We have carrots and turnips as much as we wish:
And if there's a mind for a delicate dish
We repair to the clam-banks, and there we catch fish.
Instead of pottage and puddings and custards and pies,
Our pumpkins and parsnips are common supplies;
We have pumpkins at morning and pumpkins at noon,
If it was not for pumpkins we should be undone!

If barley be wanting to make into malt,
We must be contented, and think it no fault;
For we can make liquor to sweeten our lips,
Of pumpkins and parsnips and walnut-tree chips. . . .

Now while some are going let others be coming,
For while liquor's boiling it must have a-scumming;
But I will not blame them, for birds of a feather
By seeking their fellows are flocking together.
But you whom the Lord intends hither to bring,
Forsake not the honey for fear of the sting;
But bring both a quiet and contented mind,
And all needful blessings you surely will find.

THOMAS DUDLEY

(*1576-1653*)

A New England Gentleman's Epitaph

Dim eyes, deaf ears, cold stomach show
My dissolution is in view;
Eleven times seven near lived have I,
And now God calls, I willing die:
My shuttle's shot, my race is run,
My sun is set, my deed is done;
My span is measur'd, tale is told,
My flower is faded and grown old,
My dream is vanish'd, shadow's fled,
My soul with Christ, my body dead;
Farewell dear wife, children and friends,
Hate heresy, make blessed ends;
Bear poverty, live with good men,
So shall we meet with joy again.

Let men of God in courts and churches watch
O'er such as do a toleration hatch;
Lest that ill egg bring forth a cockatrice,
To poison all with heresy and vice.
If men be left, and otherwise combine,
My epitaph's, *I died no libertine.*

ANNE BRADSTREET

(*1612-1672*)

Contemplations

Some time now past in the Autumnal Tide,
When Phœbus wanted but one hour to bed,
The trees all richly clad, yet void of pride,
Were gilded o'er by his rich golden head;
Their leaves and fruits seem'd painted, but was true
Of green, of red, of yellow, mixed hue;
Rapt were my senses at this delectable view.

I wist not what to wish; "yet sure," thought I,
"If so much excellence abide below,
How excellent is He that dwells on high,
Whose power and beauty by his works we know!
Sure He is goodness, wisdom, glory, light,
That hath his under-world so richly dight."
More Heaven than Earth was here, no winter and no night.

Then on a stately Oak I cast mine Eye,
Whose ruffling top the Clouds seem'd to aspire:
"How long since thou wast in thine Infancy?
Thy strength and stature, more thy years admire.
Hath hundred winters past since thou wast born,
Or thousand since thou brakest thy shell of horn?
If so, all these as nought Eternity doth scorn."

Then higher on the glistering Sun I gaz'd,
Whose beams was shaded by the leafy Tree.

The more I look'd the more I grew amaz'd,
And softly said: "What glory's like to thee,
Soul of this world, this Universe's Eye?
No wonder some made thee a Deity:
Had I not better known, alas, the same had I.

"Thou as a Bridegroom from thy Chamber rushes,
And as a strong man joys to run a race;
The morn doth usher thee with smiles and blushes,
The Earth reflects her glances in thy face;
Birds, insects, Animals, with Vegative,
Thy heart from death and dulness doth revive,
And in the darksome womb of fruitful nature dive.

"Thy swift Annual and diurnal Course,
Thy daily straight and yearly oblique path,
Thy pleasing fervor and thy scorching force,
All mortals here the feeling knowledge hath.
Thy presence makes it day, thy absence night;
Quaternal Seasons caused by thy might.
Hail, Creature full of sweetness, beauty, and delight!

"Art thou so full of glory that no Eye
Hath strength thy shining Rays once to behold?
And is thy splendid Throne erect so high
As to approach it can no earthly mould?
How full of glory, then, must thy Creator be
Who gave this bright light luster unto thee:
Admir'd, ador'd for ever be that Majesty!"

Silent, alone, where none or saw or heard,
In pathless paths I lead my wandering feet,

5

My humble Eyes to lofty Skies I rear'd:
To sing some Song my mazed Muse thought meet;
My great Creator I would magnify,
That nature had thus decked liberally;
But Ah, and Ah again, my imbecility!

I heard the merry Grasshopper then sing,
The black-clad Cricket bear a second part;
They kept one tune and played on the same string,
Seeming to glory in their little Art.
Shall Creatures abject thus their voices raise,
And in their kind resound their Maker's praise,
Whilst I as mute can warble forth no higher lays?

When present times look back to Ages past,
And men in being fancy those are dead,
It makes things gone perpetually to last,
And calls back months and years that long since fled;
It makes a man more aged in conceit
Than was Methuselah or's grand-sire great,
While of their persons and their acts his mind doth treat.

Sometimes in Eden fair he seems to be;
Sees glorious Adam there made Lord of all;
Fancies the Apple dangle on the Tree,
That turn'd his Sovereign to a naked thrall,
Who like a miscreant's driven from that place,
To get his bread with pain and sweat of face,
A penalty impos'd on his backsliding Race.

Here sits our Grandam in retired place,
And in her lap her bloody Cain new born;
6

The weeping Imp oft looks her in the face,
Bewails his unknown hap and fate forlorn:
His Mother sighs to think of Paradise,
And how she lost her bliss to be more wise,
Believing him that was and is Father of lies.

Here Cain and Abel come to sacrifice;
Fruits of the Earth and Fatlings each do bring:
On Abel's gift the fire descends from Skies,
But no such sign on false Cain's offering.
With sudden hateful looks he goes his ways,
Hath thousand thoughts to end his brothers days,
Upon whose blood his future good he hopes to raise.

Who fancies not his looks now at the Bar?
His face like death, his heart with horror fraught.
No Malefactor ever felt like war
When deep despair with wish of life hath fought.
Branded with guilt and crusht with treble woes,
A Vagabond to Land of Nod he goes;
A City builds, that walls might him secure from foes.

Who thinks not oft upon the Fathers' ages?
Their long descent; how nephews' sons they saw;
The starry observations of those Sages,
And how their precepts to their sons were law;
How Adam sigh'd to see his Progeny
Cloth'd all in his black sinful Livery,
Who neither guilt nor yet the punishment could fly.

Our Life compare we with their length of days;
Who to the tenth of theirs doth now arrive?

And though thus short, we shorten many ways,
Living so little while we are alive:
In eating, drinking, sleeping, vain delight,
So unawares comes on perpetual night,
And puts all pleasures vain unto eternal flight.

When I behold the heavens as in their prime,
And then the earth, though old, still clad in green
The stones and trees insensible of time,
Nor age nor wrinkle on their front are seen;
If winter come and greenness then do fade,
A Spring returns and they more youthful made;
But Man grows old, lies down, remains where once he's laid:

By birth more noble then those creatures all,
Yet seems by nature and by custom curs'd:
No sooner born, but grief and care makes fall,
That state obliterate he had at first;
Nor youth nor strength nor wisdom spring again,
Nor habitations long their names retain,
But in oblivion to the final day remain.

Shall I, then, praise the heavens, the trees, the earth,
Because their beauty and their strength last longer?
Shall I wish there or never to had birth,
Because they're bigger, and their bodies stronger?
Nay, they shall darken, perish, fade, and die,
And when unmade so ever shall they lie:
But man was made for endless immortality.

Under the cooling shadow of a stately Elm,
Close sat I by a goodly River's side,

Where gliding streams the Rocks did overwhelm;
A lonely place, with pleasures dignified.
I once that lov'd the shady woods so well
Now thought the rivers did the trees excell;
And if the sun would ever shine, there would I dwell.

While on the stealing stream I fixt mine eyes,
Which to the long'd-for Ocean held its course,
I markt nor crooks nor rubs that there did lie
Could hinder ought, but still augment its force:
"Oh happy Flood," quoth I, "that holds thy race
Till thou arrive at thy beloved place,
Nor is it rocks or shoals that can obstruct thy pace.

"Nor is't enough that thou alone may'st slide,
But hundred brooks in thy clear waves do meet;
So hand in hand along with thee they glide
To Thetis' house, where all embrace and greet:
Thou Emblem true of what I count the best,
O could I lead my Rivulets to rest,
So may we press to that vast mansion ever blest!

"Ye Fish which in this liquid Region 'bide,
That for each season have your habitation,
Now salt, now fresh, where you think best to glide
To unknown coasts to give a visitation,
In Lakes and Ponds you leave your numerous fry;
So nature taught, and yet you know not why,
You wat'ry folk that know not your felicity.

"Look how the wantons frisk to taste the air,
Then to the colder bottom straight they dive;

Eftsoon to Neptune's glassy Hall repair,
To see what trade the great ones there do drive,
Who forage o'er the spacious sea-green field
And take the trembling prey before it yield,
Whose armour is their scales, their spreading fins their shield."

While musing thus, with contemplation fed,
And thousand fancies buzzing in my brain,
The sweet-tongued Philomel percht o'er my head,
And chanted forth a most melodious strain;
Which rapt me so with wonder and delight
I judg'd my hearing better than my sight,
And wisht me wings with her a while to take my flight.

"O merry Bird," said I, "that fears no snares,
That neither toils nor hoards up in thy barn,
Feels no sad thoughts, nor 'cruciating cares
To gain more good or shun what might thee harm;
Thy clothes ne'er wear, thy meat is everywhere,
Thy bed a bough, thy drink the water clear;
Reminds not what is past, nor what's to come dost fear.

"The dawning morn with songs thou dost prevent,
Sets hundred notes unto thy feathered crew,
So each one tunes his pretty instrument
And, warbling out the old, begin anew;
And thus they pass their youth in summer season,
Then follow thee into a better Region,
Where winter's never felt by that sweet airy legion."

Man at the best a creature frail and vain,
In knowledge ignorant, in strength but weak,

Subject to sorrows, losses, sickness, pain,
Each storm his state, his mind, his body break;
From some of these he never finds cessation,
But day or night, within, without, vexation,
Troubles from foes, from friends, from dearest, near'st Relation.

And yet this sinful creature, frail and vain,
This lump of wretchedness, of sin and sorrow,
This weather-beaten vessel wrackt with pain,
Joys not in hope of an eternal morrow;
Nor all his losses, crosses, and vexation,
In weight, in frequency and long duration,
Can make him deeply groan for that divine Translation.

The Mariner that on smooth waves doth glide
Sings merrily and steers his Barque with ease,
As if he had command of wind and tide,
And now become great Master of the seas;
But suddenly a storm spoils all the sport,
And makes him long for a more quiet port,
Which, 'gainst all adverse winds, may serve for fort.

So he that saileth in this world of pleasure,
Feeding on sweets, that never bit of th' sour,
That's full of friends, of honour, and of treasure,
Fond fool, he takes this earth ev'n for heav'ns bower.
But sad affliction comes and makes him see
Here's neither honour, wealth, nor safety:
Only above is found all with security.

O Time! the fatal wrack of mortal things,
That draws oblivion's curtains over kings,

Their sumptuous monuments, men know them not,
Their names without a Record are forgot,
Their parts, their ports, their pomp's all laid in th' dust,
Nor wit nor gold nor buildings 'scape times rust:
But he whose name is grav'd in the white stone
Shall last and shine when all of these are gone.

"As Weary Pilgrim"

As weary pilgrim, now at rest,
  Hugs with delight his silent nest,
His wasted limbs now lie full soft
  That miry steps have trodden oft;
Blesses himself to think upon
  His dangers past and travails done,
The burning sun no more shall heat,
  Nor stormy rains on him shall beat;
The briars and thorns no more shall scratch,
  Nor hungry wolves at him shall catch;
He erring paths no more shall tread,
  Nor wild fruits eat, instead of bread;
For waters cold he doth not long,
  For thirst no more shall parch his tongue;
No rugged stones his feet shall gall,
  Nor stumps nor rocks cause him to fall;
All cares and fears he bids farewell,
  And means in safety now to dwell—
A pilgrim I on earth, perplexed
  With sins, with cares and sorrows vexed,
By age and pains brought to decay,
  And my clay house moldering away,

Oh, how I long to be at rest,
   And soar on high among the blest!
This body shall in silence sleep,
   Mine eyes no more shall ever weep;
No fainting fits shall me assail,
   Nor grinding pains my body frail,
With cares and fears ne'er cumbered be,
   Nor losses know, nor sorrows see.
What though my flesh shall there consume?
   It is the bed Christ did perfume;
And when a few years shall be gone
   This mortal shall be clothed upon.
A corrupt carcass down it lies,
   A glorious body it shall rise,
In weakness and dishonor sown,
   In power 'tis raised by Christ alone.
Then soul and body shall unite,
   And of their maker have the sight;
Such lasting joys shall there behold
   As ear ne'er heard nor tongue e'er told.
Lord, make me ready for that day!
   Then come, dear bridegroom, come away.

THOMAS TILLAM

(1612?-1669?)

Upon the First Sight of New England: June 29, 1638

Hail, holy land, wherein our holy Lord
Hath planted his most true and holy word.
Hail, happy people, who have dispossessed
Yourselves of friends and means to find some rest
For your poor wearied souls, oppressed of late,
For Jesus' sake, with envy, spite and hate.
To you that blessèd promise truly's given
Of sure reward, which you'll receive in heaven.
Methinks I hear the Lamb of God thus speak:
"Come, dear little flock who, for my sake,
Have left your country, dearest friends, and goods,
And hazarded your lives on raging floods,
Possess this country; free from all annoy
Here I'll be with you, here you shall enjoy
My sabbaths, sacraments, my ministry
And ordinances in their purity.
But yet beware of Satan's wily baits;
He lurks among you; cunningly he waits
To catch you from me. Live not then secure,
But fight 'gainst sin, and let your lives be pure.
Prepare to hear your sentence thus expressed:
Come ye, my servants of my Father blessed."

MICHAEL WIGGLESWORTH

(*1631-1705*)

Vanity of Vanities

Vain, frail, short liv'd and miserable Man,
Learn what thou art when thine estate is best:
A restless Wave o' th' troubled Oceàn,
A dream, a lifeless Picture finely drest:

A Wind, a Flower, a Vapor, and a Bubble,
A Wheel that stands not still, a trembling Reed,
A rolling stone, dry Dust, light Chaff, and Stubble,
A Shadow of Something, but nought indeed.

Learn what deceitful Toys, and empty things,
This World, and all its best Enjoyments be:
Out of the Earth no true Contentment springs,
But all things here are vexing Vanity.

For what is Beauty but a fading Flower?
Or what is Pleasure, but the Devil's bait,
Whereby he catcheth whom he would devour,
And multitudes of Souls doth ruinate?

And what are Friends but mortal men, as we?
Whom Death from us may quickly separate;
Or else their hearts may quite estrangèd be,
And all their love be turnèd into hate.

And what are Riches to be doted on?
Uncertain, fickle, and ensnaring things;
They draw Men's Souls into Perdition,
And when most needed take them to their wings.

Ah foolish Man! that sets his heart upon
Such empty Shadows, such wild Fowl as these,
That being gotten will be quickly gone,
And whilst they stay increase but his disease.

As in a Dropsie, drinking draughts begets,
The more he drinks, the more he still requires:
So on this World whoso affection sets,
His Wealth's increase increaseth his desires.

O happy Man, whose portion is above,
Where Floods, where Flames, where Foes cannot bereave him,
Most wretched man, that fixèd hath his love
Upon this World, that surely will deceive him.

For, what is Honor? What is Sov'reignty,
Whereto men's hearts so restlessly aspire?
Whom have they crownèd with Felicity?
When did they ever satisfy desire?

The Ear of Man with hearing is not fill'd:
To see new sights still coveteth the Eye:
The craving Stomach, though it may be stil'd,
Yet craves again without a new supply.

All Earthly things, man's Cravings answer not,
Whose little heart would all the World contain

(If all the World should fall to one man's Lot)
And notwithstanding empty still remain.

The Eastern Conqueror was said to weep,
When he the Indian Ocean did view,
To see his Conquest bounded by the Deep,
And no more Worlds remaining to subdue.

Who would that man in his Enjoyments bless,
Or envy him, or covet his estate,
Whose gettings do augment his greediness,
And make his wishes more intemperate?

Such is the wonted and the common guise
Of those on Earth that bear the greatest sway:
If with a few the case be otherwise
They seek a Kingdom that abides for ay.

Moreover they, of all the Sons of men,
That Rule, and are in highest places set,
Are most inclin'd to scorn their Brethren
And God himself (without great grace) forget.

For as the Sun doth blind the gazer's eyes,
That for a time they nought discern aright:
So Honor doth befool and blind the Wise,
And their own Lustre 'reaves them of their sight.

Great are their Dangers, manifold their Cares;
Thro which, whilst others Sleep, they scarcely Nap:
And yet are oft surprizèd unawares,
And fall unweeting into Envy's Trap!

The mean Mechanic finds his kindly rest,
All void of fear sleepeth the Country-Clown,
When greatest Princes often are distrest,
And cannot sleep upon their Beds of Down.

Could Strength or Valor men Immortalize,
Could Wealth or Honor keep them from decay,
There were some cause the same to Idolize,
And give the lie to that which I do say.

But neither can such things themselves endure
Without the hazard of a Change one hour,
Nor such as trust in them can they secure
From dismal days, or Death's prevailing pow'r.

If Beauty could the beautiful defend
From Death's dominion, then fair Absalom
Had not been brought to such a shameful end:
But fair and foul unto the Grave must come.

If Wealth or Scepters could Immortal make,
Then wealthy Croesus, wherefore art thou dead?
If Warlike force which makes the World to quake,
Then why is Julius Caesar perishèd?

Where are the Scipio's Thunderbolts of war?
Renownèd Pompey, Caesar's Enemy?
Stout Hannibal, Rome's Terror known so far?
Great Alexander, what's become of thee?

If Gifts and Bribes, Death's favor might but win,
If Power, if force, or Threat'nings might it fray,

18

All these, and more, had still surviving been:
But all are gone, for Death will have no Nay.

Such is this World with all her Pomp and Glory,
Such are the men whom worldly eyes admire:
Cut down by Time and now become a Story,
That we might after better things aspire.

Go boast thyself of what thy heart enjoys,
Vain Man! triumph in all thy worldly Bliss:
Thy best enjoyments are but Trash and Toys:
Delight thyself in that which worthless is.

JOHN SAFFIN

(*1632-1710*)

To Her, Coming Home

Sail, gentle pinnace, Zepherus doth not fail
With prosperous gales. Sail, gentle pinnace, sail.
Proud Neptune stoops and freely condescends,
For's former roughness, now to make amends.
Thetis with her green mantle sweetly glides
With smiling dimples, singing by our sides.
Sail, gentle pinnace, Zepherus doth not fail
With prosperous gales. Sail, gentle pinnace, sail!

ANONYMOUS

(SEVENTEENTH CENTURY)

Bacon's Epitaph, Made by His Man

Death, why so cruel? What! No other way
To manifest thy spleen, but thus to slay
Our hopes of safety, liberty, our all,
Which, through thy tyranny, with him must fall
To its late chaos? Had thy rigid force
Been dealt by retail, and not thus in gross,
Grief had been silent. Now we must complain,
Since thou, in him, hast more than thousand slain,
Whose lives and safeties did so much depend
On him their life, with him their lives must end.
If't be a sin to think Death bribed can be
We must be guilty; say it was bribery
Guided the fatal shaft, Virginia's foes,
To whom for secret crimes just vengeance owes
Deservèd plagues, dreading their just desert,
Corrupted Death by Paracelsian art
Him to destroy, whose well tried courage such,
Their heartless hearts, nor arms nor strength could touch.
Who now must heal those wounds or stop that blood
The Heathen made, and drew into a flood?
Who is it must plead our cause? Nor trump nor drum
Nor Deputations; these, alas! are dumb
And cannot speak. Our arms (though ne'er so strong)
Will want the aid of his commanding tongue,
Which conquered more than Caesar. He o'erthrew

Only the outward frame; this could subdue
The rugged works of nature. Souls replete
With dull chill cold, he'd animate with heat
Drawn forth of reason's limbec. In a word,
Mars and Minerva both in him concurred
For arts, for arms, whose pen and sword alike
As Cato's did, may admiration strike
Into his foes; while they confess withal
It was their guilt styled him a criminal.
Only this difference does from truth proceed:
They in the guilt, he in the name must bleed.
While none shall dare his obsequies to sing
In deserved measures; until time shall bring
Truth crowned with freedom, and from danger free
To sound his praises to posterity.
Here let him rest; while we this truth report
He's gone from hence unto a higher Court
To plead his cause, where he by this doth know
Whether to Caesar he was friend, or foe.

BENJAMIN THOMPSON

(*1642-1714*)

The Good Old Times

(*From "New England's Crisis"*)

The times wherein old Pompion was a saint,
When men fared hardly yet without complaint,
On vilest cates; the dainty Indian maize
Was eat with clam-shells out of wooden trays,
Under thatch'd huts without the cry of rent,
And the best sauce to every dish, content.
When flesh was food and hairy skins made coats,
And men as well as birds had chirping notes. . . .
Of Ceres' bounty form'd was many a knack.
Enough to fill poor Robin's Almanac.
These golden times (too fortunate to hold)
Were quickly sinned away for love of gold.
'Twas then among the bushes, not the street,
If one in place did an inferior meet,
"Good-morrow, brother, is there aught you want?
Take freely of me, what I have you ha'nt."
Plain Tom and Dick would pass as current now,
As ever since "Your Servant, Sir," and bow.
Deep-skirted doublets, puritanic capes,
Which now would render men like upright apes,
Was comelier wear, our wiser fathers thought,
Than the cast fashions from all Europe brought.
'Twas in those days an honest grace would hold

23

Till a hot pudding grew at heart a cold.
And men had better stomachs at religion
Than I to capon, turkey-cock, or pigeon;
When honest sisters met to pray, not prate,
About their own and not their neighbor's state.
During Plain Dealing's reign, that worthy stud
Of the ancient planter's race before the flood,
Then times were good, merchants cared not a rush
For other fare than johnny-cake and mush.
Although men far'd and lodg'd very hard,
Yet innocence was better than a guard.

EDWARD TAYLOR

(1642?-1729)

The Ebb and Flow

When first thou on me, Lord, wrought'st thy sweet print,
   My heart was made thy tinder box.
My 'ffections were thy tinder in't:
    Where fell thy sparks by drops.
Those holy sparks of heavenly fire that came
Did ever catch and often out would flame.

But now my heart is made thy censer trim,
   Full of thy golden altar's fire,
To offer up sweet incense in
    Unto thyself entire:
I find my tinder scarce thy sparks can feel
That drop out from thy holy flint and steel.

Hence doubts out bud for fear thy fire in me
   'S a mocking *ignis fatuus*;
Or lest thine altars fire out be,
    It's hid in ashes thus.
Yet when the bellows of thy spirit blow
Away mine ashes, then thy fire doth glow.

Upon What Base Was Fixed the Lath Wherein

Upon what base was fixed the lath wherein
He turned this glove and riggalled it so trim?
Who blew the bellows of His furnace vast?
Or held the mould wherein the world was cast?
Who laid its corner-stone? Or whose commands?
Where stand the pillars upon which it stands?
Who laced and filleted the earth so fine
With rivers like green ribbons smaragdine?
Who made the seas its selvage, and its locks
Like a quilt ball within a silver box?
Who spread its canopy? Or curtains spun?
Who in this bowling alley bowled the sun?

Housewifery: I

Make me, O Lord, Thy spinning-wheel complete.
  Thy holy Word my distaff make for me;
Make mine affections Thy swift flyers neat;
  And make my soul Thy holy spool to be;
  My conversation make to by Thy reel,
  And reel the yarn thereon spun of Thy wheel.

Make me Thy loom then; knit therein this twine;
  And make Thy Holy Spirit, Lord, wind quills.
Then weave the web Thyself. The yarn is fine.
  Thine ordinances make my fulling mills.

Then dye the same in heavenly colors choice,
All pinked with varnished flowers of paradise.

Then clothe therewith mine understanding will,
Affections, judgment, conscience, memory,
My words and actions, that their shine may fill
My ways with glory and Thee glorify.
Then mine apparel shall display before Ye
That I am clothed in holy robes for glory.

Housewifery: II

Make me thy spinning wheel of use for thee;
Thy Grace my distaff, and my heart thy spool.
Turn thou the wheel: let mine affections be
The flyers filling with thy yarn my soul.
Then weave the web of Grace in me, thy loom,
And clothe my soul therewith, its glories bloom.

Make me thy loom; thy Grace the warp therein.
My duties weave, and let thy word wind quills.
Thy shuttle shoot. Cut off the ends, my sins.
Thy Ordinances make my fulling mills,
My life thy Web: and clothe me all my days
With this gold-web of Glory, to thy praise.

Upon the Sweeping Flood

O! that I'd had a tear to've quenched that flame
Which did dissolve the Heavens above
Into those liquid drops that came
To drown our carnal love.
Our cheeks were dry and eyes refused to weep.
Tears bursting out ran down the sky's dark cheek.

Were the Heavens sick? Must we their doctors be
And physic them with pills, our sin?
To make them purge and vomit; see;
And excrements out fling?
We've grieved them by such physic that they shed
Their excrements upon our lofty heads.

What Love Is This

(From Meditations: 1)

What love is this of Thine, that cannot be
In Thine infinity, O Lord, confined,
Unless it in Thy very persons see
Infinity and finity conjoined?
What! hath Thy godhead, as not satisfied,
Married our manhood, making it its bride?

Oh, matchless love! filling heaven to the brim!
O'errunning it, all running o'er beside

This world! Nay, overflowing hell, wherein
    For Thine elect there rose a mighty tide!
    That there our veins might through Thy Person bleed
    To quench those flames that else would on us feed.

Oh! that my love might overflow my heart
    To fire the same with love! For love I would,
But oh! my straitened breast! my lifeless spark!
    My fireless flame! What chilly love and cold!
    In measure small! in manner chilly! See!
    Lord, blow the coal, Thy love enflame in me.

Oh! What a Thing Is Man

(From Meditations: 38)

Oh! What a thing is man? Lord, who am I?
    That Thou shouldst give him law (Oh! golden line)
To regulate his thoughts, words, life thereby?
    And judge him wilt thereby too in Thy time.
    A court of justice Thou in heaven hold'st
    To try his case while he's here housed in mould.

How do Thy angels lay before Thine eye
    My deeds both white and black I daily do?
How doth Thy court Thou panel'st there them try?
    But flesh complains. What right for this? Let's know.
    For right or wrong, I can't appear unto't.
    And shall a sentence pass on such a suit.

Soft; blemish not this golden bench or place.
    Here is no bribe, nor colorings to hide,

Nor pettifogger to befog the case;
    But justice hath her glory here well tried;
    Her spotless law all spotted cases tends,
    Without respect or disrespect them ends.

God's judge Himself, and Christ attorney is,
    The Holy Ghost registerer is found;
Angels the sergeants are, all creatures kiss
    The book, and do as evidence abound.
    All cases pass according to pure law,
    And in the sentence is no fret nor flaw.

What saith my soul? Here all thy deeds are tried.
    Is Christ thy advocate to plead thy cause?
Art thou His client? Such shall never slide.
    He never lost His case: He pleads such laws
As carry do the same, nor doth refuse
    The vilest sinner's case that doth Him choose.

This is His honor, not dishonor. Nay,
    No habeas corpus 'gainst His clients came.
For all their fines His purse doth make down pay.
    He non-suits Satan's suit or casts the same.
    He'll plead thy case, and not accept a fee.
    He'll plead *sub forma pauperis* for thee.

My case is bad. Lord, be my advocate.
    My sin is red; I'm under God's arrest.
Thou hast the hit of pleading; plead my state.
    Although it's bad, Thy plea will make it best.
    If Thou wilt plead my case before the King,
    I'll wagon-loads of love and glory bring.

VI

This Dove &
Olive Branch to
you
Is both a Post &
Emblem too[1]
These for M[y Dove]
Tender & Onely [Love]
Mrs. Elizabeth [Fitch][2]
at her father's house in
N[orwich]

[A] spiring Love, that Scorns to hatch a Wish
[B] eneath itselfe, the fullest, chiefest Blisse
[C] ontain'd within   Heav E ns Chrystall Pale, & Shine,
[D] ot]h wish its Object   a L w A yes; So doth mine.
[E] lec]t no more   P res S ented in desire:
[F] or H]eavens Roofe,   a Y e, lets not A wish soar higher.
[G] ot t]hough too   di M I N A N e can get to sign
[H] ear]e you, (my   FR E I ND) y^{is} stren G T h'ned Wish of mine.
[I] n d]rossy   Sil V R should,   I SH ould by this,
K eep dull my   P O S T,   and staine my   S E rious Wish.
L est wch pol L V ted bee,   or th' f E A rfull Dove
M y Post out   F O yl'd   I ru N a R ing of Love,
N ew   P O L lisht, w^{re} my   cent'red heart D o T h reek
O ut   hi G hes   T Steams of Love,   which here D oe M eet
P rese N ted   t H us y^r Heart,   LOVES RI N G   yo V 'll finde
Q uest I onlesse,   A lwayes [the] best   B E fitt   S ye minde.
R ese R ve mine   T hat. Yet let   O ur   secre T breast
S E t Love   t H e Tune which   tu N es this Ring ye B est.
H e Ring of Love my   Ple A sant   H eart must   b E E
T RVELY CONFIND WI T HIN THE TRINITIE

V { pon your Hearte (I pray you) put Loves Ring
   { nerringly; Loves Swelt [ring] Hearte herein
W { earing a True-Loves-Knot at centre's set.
   { here with I send to you an Alphabet
X { enodick whence all syllables compleat.
   { tracted are to spell what Love can speake
Y ea, see, then what I send. Yet I design
Z ion my Ring shall Licen[c]e with her Trine

[*Triangle:* The ring of love my pleasant heart mvst bee   [*Circle:* Lovs Ring I send
         Trvely confind within the Trinitie]   That hath no end]

1 These words are written inside a crude drawing of a dove holding an olive branch with which Taylor decorated this page of his manuscript.

2 Taylor's first wife, whom he married on November 5, 1674, was Elizabeth.

JOHN SECCOMB

(1708-1793)

Father Abbey's Will

To my dear wife,
My joy and life
I freely now do give her
My whole estate,
With all my plate,
Being just about to leave her

My tub of soap,
A long cart rope,
A frying pan and kettle,
An ashes pail,
A threshing flail,
An iron wedge and beetle.

Two painted chairs,
Nine warden pears,
A large old dripping platter,
This bed of hay,
On which I lay,
An old saucepan for butter.

A little mug,
A two-quart jug,
A bottle full of brandy,
A looking glass,

To see your face
You'll find it very handy.

A musket true
As ever flew,
A pound of shot and wallet,
A leather sash,
My calabash,
My powder horn and bullet.

An old sword blade,
A garden spade,
A hoe, a rake, a ladder,
A wooden can,
A close-stool pan,
A clyster-pipe and bladder.

A greasy hat,
My old ram cat,
A yard and half of linen,
A woolen fleece,
A pot of grease,
In order for your spinning.

A small tooth comb,
An ashen broom,
A candlestick and hatchet,
A coverlid
Striped down with red,
A bag of rags to patch it.

A ragged mat,
A tub of fat,

A book put out by Bunyan,
Another book
By Robin Cook,
A skein or two of spunyarn.

An old black muff,
Some garden stuff,
A quantity of borage,
Some devil's weed
And burdock seed,
To season well your porridge.

A chafing dish,
With one salt fish,
If I am not mistaken,
A leg of pork,
A broken fork,
And half a flitch of bacon.

A spinning wheel,
One peck of meal,
A knife without a handle,
A rusty lamp,
Two quarts of samp,
And half a tallow candle.

My pouch and pipes,
Two oxen tripes,
An oaken dish well carved,
My little dog
And spotted hog,
With two young pigs just starved.

This is my store,
I have no more,
I heartily do give it,
My years are spun,
My days are done,
And so I think to leave it.

FRANCIS HOPKINSON

(*1737-1791*)

The Battle of the Kegs

Gallants attend and hear a friend
  Trill forth harmonious ditty,
Strange things I'll tell which late befell
  In Philadelphia city.

'Twas early day, as poets say,
  Just when the sun was rising,
A soldier stood on a log of wood,
  And saw a thing surprising.

As in amaze he stood to gaze,
  The truth can't be denied, sir,
He spied a score of kegs or more
  Come floating down the tide, sir.

A sailor too in jerkin blue,
  This strange appearance viewing,
First damned his eyes, in great surprise,
  Then said, "Some mischief's brewing.

"These kegs, I'm told, the rebels hold,
  Packed up like pickled herring;
And they're come down to attack the town,
  In this new way of ferrying."

The soldier flew, the sailor too,
  And scared almost to death, sir,
Wore out their shoes, to spread the news,
  And ran till out of breath, sir.

Now up and down throughout the town,
  Most frantic scenes were acted;
And some ran here, and others there,
  Like men almost distracted.

Some fire cried, which some denied,
  But said the earth had quakéd;
And girls and boys, with hideous noise,
  Ran through the streets half naked.

Sir William he, snug as a flea,
  Lay all this time a snoring,
Nor dreamed of harm as he lay warm,
  In bed with Mrs. Loring.

Now in a fright, he starts upright,
  Awaked by such a clatter;
He rubs both eyes, and boldly cries,
  "For God's sake, what's the matter?"

At his bedside he then espied,
  Sir Erskine at command, sir,
Upon one foot he had one boot,
  And th'other in his hand, sir.

"Arise, arise," Sir Erskine cries,
  "The rebels—more's the pity,

Without a boat are all afloat,
    And ranged before the city.

"The motley crew, in vessels new,
    With Satan for their guide, sir,
Packed up in bags, or wooden kegs,
    Come driving down the tide, sir.

"Therefore prepare for bloody war,
    These kegs must all be routed,
Or surely we despised shall be,
    And British courage doubted."

The royal band now ready stand
    All ranged in dread array, sir,
With stomach stout to see it out,
    And make a bloody day, sir.

The cannons roar from shore to shore,
    The small arms make a rattle;
Since wars began I'm sure no man
    E'er saw so strange a battle.

The rebel dales, the rebel vales,
    With rebel trees surrounded,
The distant woods, the hills and floods,
    With rebel echoes sounded.

The fish below swam to and fro,
    Attacked from every quarter;
Why sure, thought they, the devil's to pay,
    'Mongst folks above the water.

The kegs, 'tis said, though strongly made,
    Of rebel staves and hoops, sir,
Could not oppose their powerful foes,
    The conquering British troops, sir.

From morn to night these men of might
    Displayed amazing courage;
And when the sun was fairly down,
    Retired to sup their porridge.

A hundred men with each a pen,
    Or more upon my word, sir,
It is most true would be too few,
    Their valour to record, sir.

Such feats did they perform that day,
    Against these wicked kegs, sir,
That years to come, if they get home,
    They'll make their boasts and brags, sir.

PHILIP FRENEAU

(1752-1832)

From "The House of Night"

O'er a dark field I held my dubious way
Where Jack-a-lantern walked his lonely round,
Beneath my feet substantial darkness lay,
And screams were heard from the distempered ground.

Nor looked I back, till to a far-off wood
Trembling with fear, my weary feet had sped—
Dark was the night, but at the enchanted dome
I saw the infernal windows flaming red.

And from within the howls of Death I heard,
Cursing the dismal night that gave him birth,
Damning his ancient sire, and mother sin,
Who, at the gates of hell, accursèd, brought him forth.

(For fancy gave to my enraptured soul
An eagle's eye, with keenest glance to see,
And bade those distant sounds distinctly roll,
Which, waking, never had affected me.)

Oft his pale breast, with cruel hands he smote,
And tearing from his limbs a winding sheet,
Roared to the black skies, while the woods around,
As wicked as himself, his words repeat.

40

Thrice toward the skies his meagre arms he reared,
Invoked all hell and thunders on his head,
Bid lightning fly, earth yawn, and tempests roar,
And the sea wrap him in its oozy bed.

"My life for one cool draught!—O, fetch your springs,
"Can one unfeeling to my woes be found!
"No friendly visage comes to my relief,
"But ghosts impend and spectres hover round.

"Though humbled now, disheartened and distressed,
"Yet, when admitted to the peaceful ground,
"With heroes, kings, and conquerors, I shall rest,
"Shall sleep as safely, and perhaps as sound."

The Indian Burying Ground

In spite of all the learned have said,
    I still my old opinion keep;
The posture, that we give the dead,
    Points out the soul's eternal sleep.

Not so the ancients of these lands—
    The Indian, when from life released,
Again is seated with his friends,
    And shares again the joyous feast.

His imaged birds, and painted bowl,
    And venison, for a journey dressed,
Bespeak the nature of the soul,
    Activity, that knows no rest.

41

His bow, for action ready bent,
   And arrows, with a head of stone,
Can only mean that life is spent,
   And not the old ideas gone.

Thou, stranger, that shalt come this way,
   No fraud upon the dead commit—
Observe the swelling turf, and say
   They do not lie, but here they sit.

Here still a lofty rock remains,
   On which the curious eye may trace
(Now wasted, half, by wearing rains)
   The fancies of a ruder race.

Here still an aged elm aspires,
   Beneath whose far-projecting shade
(And which the shepherd still admires)
   The children of the forest played!

There oft a restless Indian queen
   (Pale Shebah, with her braided hair)
And many a barbarous form is seen
   To chide the man that lingers there.

By midnight moons, o'er moistening dews;
   In habit for the chase arrayed,
The hunter still the deer pursues,
   The hunter and the deer, a shade!

And long shall timorous fancy see
   The painted chief, and pointed spear,

And Reason's self shall bow the knee
To shadows and delusions here.

Song of Thyrsis

The turtle on yon withered bough,
    That lately mourned her murdered mate,
Has found another comrade now—
    Such changes all await!
Again her drooping plume is drest,
Again she's willing to be blest
And takes her lover to her nest.

If nature has decreed it so
With all above, and all below,
Let us like them forget our woe,
    And not be killed with sorrow.
If I should quit your arms to-night
And chance to die before 't was light,
I would advise you—and you might—
    Love again to-morrow.

On Observing a Large Red-streak Apple

In spite of ice, in spite of snow,
In spite of all the winds that blow,
In spite of hail and biting frost,
Suspended here I see you toss'd;
You still retain your wonted hold
Though days are short and nights are cold.

43

Amidst this system of decay
How could you have one wish to stay?
If fate or fancy kept you there
They meant you for a Solitaire.

Were it not better to descend,
Or in the cider mill to end
Than thus to shiver in the storm
And not a leaf to keep you warm—
A moment, then, had buried all,
Nor you have doomed so late a fall.

But should the stem to which you cling
Uphold you to another spring,
Another race would round you rise
And view the stranger with surprise,
And, peeping from the blossoms say
Away, old dotard, get away!

Alas! small pleasure can there be
To dwell, a hermit, on the tree—
Your old companions, all, are gone,
Have dropt, and perished, every one;
You only stay to face the blast,
A sad memento of the past.

Would fate or nature hear my prayer,
I would your bloom of youth repair
I would the wrongs of time restrain
And bring your blossom state again:
But fate and nature both say no;
And you, though late must perish too.

What can we say, what can we hope?
Ere from the branch I see you drop,
All I can do, all in my power
Will be to watch your parting hour:
When from the branch I see you fall,
A grave we dig a-south the wall.

There you shall sleep till from your core,
Of youngsters rises three or four;
These shall salute the coming spring
And red streaks to perfection bring
When years have brought them to their prime
And they shall have their summers time:
This, this is all you can attain,
And thus, I bid you, live again!

On the Death of Benjamin Franklin

Thus, some tall tree that long hath stood
The glory of its native wood,
By storms destroyed, or length of years,
Demand the tribute of our tears.

The pile, that took long time to raise,
To dust returns by slow decays;
But, when its destined years are o'er,
We must regret the loss once more.

So long accustomed to your aid,
The world laments your exit made;

So long befriended by your art,
Philosopher, 't is hard to part!—

When monarchs tumble to the ground
Successors easily are found;
But, matchless Franklin! what a few
Can hope to rival such as you,
Who seized from kings their sceptered pride,
And turned the lightning's darts aside!

Stanzas

Occasioned by the Ruins of a Country Inn,
Unroofed and Blown Down in a Storm

Where now these mingled ruins lie
A Temple once to Bacchus rose,
Beneath whose roof, aspiring high,
Full many a guest forgot his woes:

No more this dome, by tempests torn,
Affords a social safe retreat;
But ravens here, with eye forlorn,
And clustering bats henceforth shall meet.

The Priestess of this ruin'd shrine,
Unable to survive the stroke,
Presents no more the ruddy wine,
Her glasses gone, her china broke.

The friendly Host, whose social hand
Accosted strangers at the door.
Has left at length his wonted stand,
And greets the weary guest no more.

Old creeping time, that brings decay,
Might yet have spar'd these mouldering walls,
Alike beneath whose potent sway
A temple or a tavern falls.

Is this the place where mirth and joy,
Coy nymphs and sprightly lads were found?
Alas! no more the nymphs are coy,
No more the flowing bowls go round.

Is this the place where festive song
Deceiv'd the wintry hours away?
No more the swains the tune prolong,
No more the maidens join the lay:

Is this the place where Chloe slept
In downy beds of blue and green?
Dame Nature here no vigils kept,
No cold, unfeeling guards were seen.

'Tis gone!—and Chloe tempts no more,
Deep, unrelenting silence reigns;
Of all that pleas'd, that charm'd before,
The tottering chimney scarce remains!

Ye tyrant winds, whose ruffian blast
From locks and hinges rent the door.

And all the roof to ruin cast,
The roof that sheltered us before,

Your wrath appeased, I pray be kind
If Mopsus should the dome renew;
That we again may quaff his wine,
Again collect our jovial crew.

To a Honey Bee

Thou, born to sip the lake or spring,
  Or quaff the waters of the stream,
Why hither come, on vagrant wing?
  Does Bacchus tempting seem—
    Did he for you this glass prepare?
    Will I admit you to a share?

Did storms harass or foes perplex,
  Did wasps or king-birds bring dismay—
Did wars distress, or labors vex,
  Or did you miss your way?
    A better seat you could not take
    Than on the margin of this lake.

Welcome!—I hail you to my glass:
  All welcome here you find;
Here let the cloud of trouble pass,
  Here be all care resigned.
    This fluid never fails to please,
    And drown the griefs of men or bees.

What forced you here we cannot know,
   And you will scarcely tell,
But cheery we would have you go
   And bid a glad farewell:
      On lighter wings we bid you fly—
      Your dart will now all foes defy.

Yet take not, oh! too deep a drink,
   And in this ocean die;
Here bigger bees than you might sink,
   Even bees full six feet high.
      Like Pharaoh, then, you would be said
      To perish in a sea of red.

Do as you please, your will is mine;
   Enjoy it without fear,
And your grave will be this glass of wine,
   Your epitaph—a tear;
      Go, take your seat in Charon's boat;
      We'll tell the hive, you died afloat.

JOEL BARLOW

(*1754-1812*)

Hymn to Peace

Hail, sacred Peace, who claim'st thy bright abode
'Mid circling saints that grace the throne of God,
Before his arm, around this shapeless earth,
Stretch'd the wide heav'ns and gave to nature birth;
Ere morning stars his glowing chambers hung,
Or songs of gladness woke an angel's tongue;
Veiled in the brightness of th' Almighty's mind,
In blessed repose thy placid form reclined;
Borne through the heaven, with his creating voice,
Thy presence bade the unfolding worlds rejoice;
Gave to seraphic hearts their sounding lays,
Their joy to angels and to men their praise.

From scenes of blood, these beauteous shores that stain,
From gasping fiends that press the sanguine plain,
From fields, long taught in vain thy flight to mourn,
I rise, delightful power, and greet thy glad return.
Too long the groans of death and battle's bray
Have rung discordant through the unpleasing lay.
Let pity's tear its balmy fragrance shed,
O'er heroes' wounds and patriot warriors dead:
Accept, departed shades, these grateful sighs,
Your fond attendants to the approving skies.
But now the untuneful trump shall grate no more,
Ye silver streams, no longer swell with gore;

Bear from your beauteous banks the crimson stain,
With yon retiring navies to the main;
While other views unfolding on my eyes,
And happier themes bid bolder numbers rise.
Bring, bounteous Peace, in thy celestial throng,
Life to my soul, and rapture to my song.
Give me to trace, with pure unclouded ray,
The arts and virtues that attend thy sway;
To see thy blissful charms that here descend,
Thro' distant realms and endless years extend.

The Pudding Praised

(From *The Hasty Pudding*: *Canto* 1)

E'en in thy native regions, how I blush
To hear the Pennsylvanians call thee *Mush*!
On Hudson's banks, while men of Belgic spawn
Insult and eat thee by the name *Suppawn*.
All spurious appellations, void of truth;
I've better known thee from my earliest youth:
Thy name is *Hasty Pudding*! thus my sire
Was wont to greet thee fuming from his fire;
And while he argued in thy just defense
With logic clear he thus explained the sense:
"In haste the boiling caldron, o'er the blaze,
Receives and cooks the ready powdered maize;
In haste 'tis served, and then in equal haste,
With cooling milk, we make the sweet repast.
No carving to be done, no knife to grate
The tender ear and wound the stony plate;

51

But the smooth spoon, just fitted to the lip,
And taught with art the yielding mass to dip,
By frequent journeys to the bowl well stored,
Performs the hasty honors of the board."
Such is thy name, significant and clear,
A name, a sound to every Yankee dear,
But most to me, whose heart and palate chaste
Preserve my pure, hereditary taste.

There are who strive to stamp with disrepute
The luscious food, because it feeds the brute;
In tropes of high-strained wit, while gaudy prigs
Compare thy nursling, man, to pampered pigs;
With sovereign scorn I treat the vulgar jest,
Nor fear to share thy bounties with the beast.
What though the generous cow gives me to quaff
The milk nutritious: am I then a calf?
Or can the genus of the noisy swine,
Though nursed on pudding, thence lay claim to mine?
Sure the sweet song I fashion to thy praise,
Runs more melodious than the notes they raise.

My song, resounding in its grateful glee,
No merit claims: I praise myself in thee.
My father loved thee through his length of days!
For thee his fields were shaded o'er with maize;
From thee what health, what vigor he possessed,
Ten sturdy freemen from his loins attest;
Thy constellation ruled my natal morn,
And all my bones were made of Indian corn.
Delicious grain, whatever form it take,
To roast or boil, to smother or to bake,

In every dish 'tis welcome still to me,
But most, my Hasty Pudding, most in thee.

Let the green succotash with thee contend;
Let beans and corn their sweetest juices blend;
Let butter drench them in its yellow tide,
And a long slice of bacon grace their side;
Not all the plate, how famed soe'er it be,
Can please my palate like a bowl of thee.
Some talk of hoe-cake, fair Virginia's pride!
Rich johnny-cake this mouth has often tried;
Both please me well, their virtues much the same,
Alike their fabric, as allied their fame,
Except in dear New England, where the last
Receives a dash of pumpkin in the paste,
To give it sweetness and improve the taste.
But place them all before me, smoking hot,
The big, round dumpling, rolling from the pot;
The pudding of the bag, whose quivering breast,
With suet lined, leads on the Yankee feast;
The charlotte brown, within whose crusty sides
A belly soft the pulpy apple hides;
The yellow bread whose face like amber glows,
And all of Indian that the bakepan knows—
You tempt me not, my favorite greets my eyes,
To that loved bowl my spoon by instinct flies.

The Pudding Prepared

(From *The Hasty Pudding*: *Canto* III)

The days grow short; but, though the falling sun
To the glad swain proclaims his day's work done,
Night's pleasing shade his various tasks prolong,
And yield new subjects to my various song.
For now, the corn-house filled, the harvest home,
The invited neighbors to the husking come;
A frolic scene, where work, and mirth, and play,
Unite their charms to chase the hours away.

Where the huge heap lies centered in the hall,
The lamp suspended from the cheerful wall,
Brown, corn-fed nymphs, and strong, hard-handed beaux,
Alternate ranged, extend in circling rows,
Assume their seats, the solid mass attack;
The dry husks rustle, and the corncobs crack;
The song, the laugh, alternate notes resound,
And the sweet cider trips in silence round.

The laws of husking every wight can tell;
And sure no laws he ever keeps so well:
For each red ear a general kiss he gains,
With each smut ear she smuts the luckless swains;
But when to some sweet maid a prize is cast,
Red as her lips and taper as her waist,
She walks the round and culls one favored beau,

Who leaps the luscious tribute to bestow.
Various the sport, as are the wits and brains
Of well-pleased lasses and contending swains;
Till the vast mound of corn is swept away,
And he that gets the last ear wins the day.

Meanwhile, the housewife urges all her care,
The well-earned feast to hasten and prepare.
The sifted meal already waits her hand,
The milk is strained, the bowls in order stand,
The fire flames high; and as a pool—that takes
The headlong stream that o'er the milldam breaks—
Foams, roars, and rages with incessant toils,
So the vexed caldron rages, roars, and boils.

First with clean salt she seasons well the food,
Then strews the flour, and thickens all the flood.
Long o'er the simmering fire she lets it stand;
To stir it well demands a stronger hand;
The husband takes his turn: and round and round
The ladle flies; at last the toil is crowned;
When to the board the thronging huskers pour,
And take their seats as at the corn before.

I leave them to their feast. There still belong
More useful matters to my faithful song.
For rules there are, though ne'er unfolded yet,
Nice rules and wise, how pudding should be ate.

Some with molasses line the luscious treat,
And mix, like bards, the useful with the sweet.
A wholesome dish, and well deserving praise,

A great resource in those bleak wintry days,
When the chilled earth lies buried deep in snow,
And raging Boreas dries the shivering cow.

  Blest cow! thy praise shall still my notes employ,
Great source of health, the only source of joy;
Mother of Egypt's god—but sure, for me,
Were I to leave my God, I'd worship thee.
How oft thy teats these pious hands have pressed!
How oft thy bounties proved my only feast!
How oft I've fed thee with my favorite grain!
And roared, like thee, to see thy children slain!

  Ye swains who know her various worth to prize,
Ah! house her well from winter's angry skies.
Potatoes, pumpkins, should her sadness cheer,
Corn from your crib, and mashes from your beer;
When spring returns, she'll well acquit the loan,
And nurse at once your infants and her own.
Milk them with pudding I should always choose;
To this in future I confine my muse,
Till she in haste some further hints unfold,
Well for the young, nor useless to the old.
First in your bowl the milk abundant take,
Then drop with care along the silver lake
Your flakes of pudding; these at first will hide
Their little bulk beneath the swelling tide;
But when their growing mass no more can sink,
When the soft island looms above the brink,
Then check your hand; you've got the portion due;
So taught our sires, and what they taught is true.

The Pudding Eaten

(From *The Hasty Pudding*: *Canto* III)

There is a choice in spoons. Though small appear
The nice distinction, yet to me 'tis clear.
The deep-bowled Gallic spoon, contrived to scoop
In ample draughts the thin, diluted soup,
Performs not well in those substantial things,
Whose mass adhesive to the metal clings;
Where the strong labial muscles must embrace
The gentle curve, and sweep the hollow space
With ease to enter and discharge the freight,
A bowl less concave, but still more dilate,
Becomes the pudding best. The shape, the size,
A secret rests, unknown to vulgar eyes.
Experienced feeders can alone impart
A rule so much above the lore of art.
These tuneful lips that thousand spoons have tried,
With just precision could the point decide,
Though not in song; the muse but poorly shines
In cones, and cubes, and geometric lines;
Yet the true form, as near as she can tell,
Is that small section of a goose-egg shell,
Which in two equal portions shall divide
The distance from the center to the side.

Fear not to slaver; 'tis no deadly sin.
Like the free Frenchman, from your joyous chin
Suspend the ready napkin; or, like me,
Poise with one hand your bowl upon your knee;

Just in the zenith your wise head project,
Your full spoon, rising in a line direct,
Bold as a bucket, heeds no drops that fall;
The wide-mouthed bowl will surely catch them all!

Freedom

Sun of the moral world; effulgent source
Of man's best wisdom and his steadiest force,
Soul-searching Freedom! here assume thy stand,
And radiate hence to every distant land;
Point out and prove how all the scenes of strife,
The shock of states, the impassion'd broils of life,
Spring from unequal sway; and how they fly
Before the splendour of thy peaceful eye;
Unfold at last the genuine social plan,
The mind's full scope, the dignity of man,
Bold nature bursting through her long disguise,
And nations daring to be just and wise.
Yes! righteous Freedom, heaven and earth and sea
Yield or withhold their various gifts for thee;
Protected Industry beneath thy reign
Leads all the virtues in her filial train;
Courageous Probity, with brow serene,
And Temperance calm presents her placid mien;
Contentment, Moderation, Labor, Art,
Mould the new man and humanize his heart;
To public plenty private ease dilates,
Domestic peace to harmony of states.

Protected Industry, careering far,
Detects the cause and cures the rage of war,
And sweeps, with forceful arm, to their last graves,
Kings from the earth and pirates from the waves.

ROYALL TYLER

(*1757-1826*)

Independence Day

Squeak the fife, and beat the drum,
Independence Day is come!
Let the roasting pig be bled.
Quick, twist off the cockerel's head.
Quickly rub the pewter platter;
Heap the nutcakes, fried in butter.
Set the cups and beaker glass,
The pumpkin and the apple sauce;
Send the keg to shop for brandy;
Maple sugar we have handy.
Independent, staggering Dick,
A noggin mix of "swingeing thick";
Sal, put on your russel skirt,
Jotham, get your *boughten* shirt,
To-day we dance to tiddle-diddle.
Here comes Sambo with his fiddle;
Sambo, take a dram of whisky
And play up Yankee Doodle frisky.
Moll, come leave your witched tricks,
And let us have a reel of six.
Father and Mother shall make two;
Sal, Moll, and I stand all a-row;
Sambo, play and dance with quality;
This is the day of blest equality.
Father and mother are but men,

And Sambo—is a citizen.
Come foot it, Sal—Moll, figure in,
And mother, you dance up to him;
Now saw as fast as e'er you can do,
And father, you cross o'er to Sambo.
—Thus we dance, and thus we play,
On glorious Independence Day—
Rub more rosin on your bow,
And let us have another go.

. . . .

Thus we drink and dance away
This glorious Independence Day!

JOHN QUINCY ADAMS

(1767-1848)

To the Sun-Dial

Under the Window of the Hall of the House
of Representatives of the United States

Thou silent herald of Time's silent flight!
  Say, could'st thou speak, what warning voice were thine?
  Shade, who canst only show how others shine!
Dark, sullen witness of resplendent light
In day's broad glare, and when the moontide bright
  Of laughing fortune sheds the ray divine,
  Thy ready favors cheer us—but decline
The clouds of morning and the gloom of night.
Yet are thy counsels faithful, just, and wise;
  They bid us seize the moments as they pass—
Snatch the retrieveless sunbeam as it flies,
  Nor lose one sand of life's revolving glass—
Aspiring still, with energy sublime,
By virtuous deeds to give eternity to Time.

JOSEPH HOPKINSON

(*1770-1842*)

Hail, Columbia

Hail, Columbia! happy land!
Hail, ye heroes! heaven-born band!
　Who fought and bled in Freedom's cause,
And when the storm of war was gone,
Enjoyed the peace your valor won.
　Let independence be our boast,
　Ever mindful what it cost;
　Ever grateful for the prize,
　Let its altar reach the skies.

　　Firm, united, let us be,
　　Rallying round our Liberty;
　　As a band of brothers joined,
　　Peace and safety we shall find.

Immortal patriots! rise once more:
Defend your rights, defend your shore:
　Let no rude foe, with impious hand,
Invade the shrine where sacred lies
Of toil and blood the well-earned prize.
　While offering peace sincere and just,
　In Heaven we place a manly trust,
　That truth and justice will prevail,
　And every scheme of bondage fail.

Sound, sound, the trump of Fame!
Let Washington's great name
  Ring through the world with loud applause;
Let every clime to Freedom dear,
Listen with a joyful ear.
  With equal skill, and godlike power,
  He governed in the fearful hour
  Of horrid war; or guides, with ease,
  The happier times of honest peace.

Behold the chief who now commands,
Once more to serve his country, stands—
  The rock on which the storm will beat;
But, armed in virtue firm and true,
His hopes are fixed on heaven and you.
  When hope was sinking in dismay,
  And glooms obscured Columbia's day,
  His steady mind, from changes free,
  Resolved on death or liberty.

    Firm, united, let us be,
    Rallying round our Liberty;
    As a band of brothers joined,
    Peace and safety we shall find.

FRANCIS SCOTT KEY

(*1779-1843*)

The Star-Spangled Banner

Oh, say, can you see, by the dawn's early light,
  What so proudly we hailed at the twilight's last gleaming,
Whose broad stripes and bright stars through the perilous fight,
  O'er the ramparts we watched were so gallantly streaming?
And the rockets' red glare, the bombs bursting in air,
Gave proof through the night that our flag was still there.
Oh, say, does that star-spangled banner yet wave
O'er the land of the free, and the home of the brave?

On the shore, dimly seen through the mists of the deep,
  Where the foe's haughty host in dread silence reposes,
What is that which the breeze, o'er the towering steep,
  As it fitfully blows, half conceals, half discloses?
Now it catches the gleam of the morning's first beam,
In full glory reflected, now shines on the stream.
'Tis the star-spangled banner; oh, long may it wave
O'er the land of the free, and the home of the brave!

And where is that band who so vauntingly swore
  That the havoc of war and the battle's confusion
A home and a country should leave us no more?
  Their blood has washed out their foul footsteps' pollution.
No refuge could save the hireling and slave
From the terror of flight, or the gloom of the grave:

And the star-spangled banner in triumph doth wave
O'er the land of the free, and the home of the brave!

Oh! thus be it ever when freemen shall stand
   Between their loved homes and the war's desolation!
Blest with victory and peace, may the heaven-rescued land
   Praise the Power that hath made and preserved us a nation!
Then conquer we must, for our cause it is just,
And this be our motto: "In God is our trust!"
And the star-spangled banner in triumph shall wave,
O'er the land of the free, and the home of the brave!

SAMUEL WOODWORTH

(1785-1842)

The Bucket

How dear to this heart are the scenes of my childhood,
　When fond recollection presents them to view!
The orchard, the meadow, the deep-tangled wild-wood,
　And every loved spot which my infancy knew!
The wide-spreading pond, and the mill that stood by it,
　The bridge, and the rock where the cataract fell,
The cot of my father, the dairy-house nigh it,
　And e'en the rude bucket that hung in the well—
The old oaken bucket, the iron-bound bucket,
The moss-covered bucket which hung in the well.

That moss-covered vessel I hailed as a treasure,
　For often at noon, when returned from the field,
I found it the source of an exquisite pleasure,
　The purest and sweetest that nature can yield.
How ardent I seized it, with hands that were glowing,
　And quick to the white-pebbled bottom it fell;
Then soon, with the emblem of truth overflowing,
　And dripping with coolness, it rose from the well—
The old oaken bucket, the iron-bound bucket,
The moss-covered bucket arose from the well.

How sweet from the green mossy brim to receive it,
　As poised on the curb it inclined to my lips!
Not a full blushing goblet could tempt me to leave it,

The brightest that beauty or revelry sips.
And now, far removed from the loved habitation,
   The tear of regret will intrusively swell,
As fancy reverts to my father's plantation,
   And sighs for the bucket that hangs in the well—
The old oaken bucket, the iron-bound bucket,
The moss-covered bucket that hangs in the well!

JOHN PIERPONT

(*1785-1866*)

Whittling

The Yankee boy, before he's sent to school,
Well knows the mysteries of that magic tool,
The pocket-knife. To that his wistful eye
Turns, while he hears his mother's lullaby;
His hoarded cents he gladly gives to get it,
Then leaves no stone unturned till he can whet it;
And in the education of the lad
No little part that implement hath had.
His pocket-knife to the young whittler brings
A growing knowledge of material things.

Projectiles, music, and the sculptor's art,
His chestnut whistle and his shingle dart,
His elder popgun with its hickory rod,
Its sharp explosion and rebounding wad,
His cornstalk fiddle, and the deeper tone
That murmurs from his pumpkin-stalk trombone,
Conspire to teach the boy. To these succeed
His bow, his arrow of a feathered seed,
His windmill, raised the passing breeze to win,
His water-wheel, that turns upon a pin;
Or, if his father lives upon the shore,
You'll see his ship, "beam ends upon the floor,"
Full rigged with raking masts, and timbers stanch,
And waiting near the wash-tub for a launch.

Thus by his genius and his jack-knife driven,
Ere long he'll solve you any problem given;
Make any gimcrack musical or mute,
A plough, a couch, an organ or a flute;
Make you a locomotive or a clock,
Cut a canal, or build a floating-dock,
Or lead forth Beauty from a marble block;—
Make anything in short, for sea or shore,
From a child's rattle to a seventy-four;—
Make it, said I—Ay, when he undertakes it,
He'll make the thing and the machine that makes it.

And when the thing is made,—whether it be
To move on earth, in air, or on the sea;
Whether on water, o'er the waves to glide,
Or upon land to roll, revolve, or slide;
Whether to whirl or jar, to strike or ring,
Whether it be a piston or a spring,
Wheel, pulley, tube sonorous, wood or brass,
The thing designed shall surely come to pass;
For, when his hand's upon it, you may know
That there's go in it, and he'll make it go.

The Pilgrim Fathers

The Pilgrim Fathers,—where are they?
  The waves that brought them o'er
Still roll in the bay, and throw their spray
  As they break along the shore;
Still roll in the bay, as they rolled that day
  When the Mayflower moored below;

When the sea around was black with storms,
   And white the shore with snow.

The mists that wrapped the Pilgrim's sleep
   Still brood upon the tide;
And his rocks yet keep their watch by the deep
   To stay its waves of pride.
But the snow-white sail that he gave to the gale,
   When the heavens looked dark, is gone,—
As an angel's wing through an opening cloud
   Is seen, and then withdrawn.

The pilgrim exile,—sainted name!
   The hill whose icy brow
Rejoiced, when he came, in the morning's flame,
   In the morning's flame burns now.
And the moon's cold light, as it lay that night
   On the hillside and the sea,
Still lies where he laid his houseless head,—
   But the Pilgrim! where is he?

The Pilgrim Fathers are at rest:
   When summer's throned on high,
And the world's warm breast is in verdure drest,
   Go, stand on the hill where they lie.
The earliest ray of the golden day
   On that hallowed spot is cast;
And the evening sun, as he leaves the world,
   Looks kindly on that spot last.

The Pilgrim spirit has not fled:
   It walks in noon's broad light;

71

And it watches the bed of the glorious dead,
  With the holy stars by night.
It watches the bed of the brave who have bled,
  And still guard this ice-bound shore,
Till the waves of the bay, where the Mayflower lay,
  Shall foam and freeze no more.

Warren's Address at Bunker Hill

Stand! the ground's your own, my braves!
Will ye give it up to slaves?
Will ye look for greener graves?
  Hope ye mercy still?
What's the mercy despots feel?
Hear it in that battle-peal!
Read it in yon bristling steel!
  Ask it—ye who will.

Fear ye foes who kill for hire?
Will ye to your homes retire?
Look behind you—they're afire!
  And, before you, see
Who have done it! From the vale
On they come—and will ye quail?
Leaden rain and iron hail
  Let their welcome be!

In the God of battles trust.
Die we may, and die we must.
But, O, where can dust to dust
  Be consigned so well

As where heaven its dews shall shed
On the martyred patriot's bed,
And the rocks shall raise their head
    Of his deeds to tell.

RICHARD HENRY DANA

(*1787-1879*)

The Little Beach Bird

Thou little bird, thou dweller by the sea,
　Why takest thou its melancholy voice?
　　Why with that boding cry
　　O'er the waves dost thou fly?
O, rather, bird, with me
　Through the fair land rejoice!

Thy flitting form comes ghostly dim and pale,
　As driven by a beating storm at sea;
　　Thy cry is weak and scared,
　　As if thy mates had shared
The doom of us. Thy wail—
　What does it bring to me?

Thou call'st along the sand, and haunt'st the surge,
　Restless and sad; as if, in strange accord
　　With motion and with roar
　　Of waves that drive to shore,
One spirit did ye urge—
　The Mystery—the Word.

Of thousands thou both sepulchre and pall,
　Old ocean, art! A requiem o'er the dead,
　　From out thy gloomy cells,
　　A tale of mourning tells,—

Tells of man's woe and fall,
  His sinless glory fled.

Then turn thee, little bird, and take thy flight
  Where the complaining sea shall sadness bring
    Thy spirit nevermore.
    Come, quit with me the shore,
For gladness and the light,
  Where birds of summer sing.

RICHARD HENRY WILDE

(1789-1847)

My Life is Like the Summer Rose

My life is like the summer rose,
  That opens to the morning sky,
But, ere the shades of evening close,
  Is scattered on the ground—to die!
Yet on the rose's humble bed
The sweetest dews of night are shed,
As if she wept the waste to see—
But none shall weep a tear for me!

My life is like the autumn leaf
  That trembles in the moon's pale ray:
Its hold is frail—its date is brief,
  Restless—and soon to pass away!
Yet, ere that leaf shall fall and fade,
The parent tree will mourn its shade,
The winds bewail the leafless tree—
But none shall breathe a sigh for me!

My life is like the prints, which feet
  Have left on Tampa's desert strand;
Soon as the rising tide shall beat,
  All trace will vanish from the sand;
Yet, as if grieving to efface
All vestige of the human race,
On that lone shore loud moans the sea—
But none, alas! shall mourn for me!

FITZ-GREENE HALLECK

(*1790-1867*)

On the Death of Joseph Rodman Drake[1]

Green be the turf above thee,
   Friend of my better days!
None knew thee but to love thee,
   Nor named thee but to praise.

Tears fell when thou wert dying,
   From eyes unused to weep,
And long, where thou art lying,
   Will tears the cold turf steep.

When hearts, whose truth was proven,
   Like thine, are laid in earth,
There should a wreath be woven
   To tell the world their worth;

And I who woke each morrow
   To clasp thy hand in mine,
Who shared thy joy and sorrow,
   Whose weal and woe were thine;

It should be mine to braid it
   Around thy faded brow,
But I've in vain essayed it,
   And feel I cannot now.

[1] For the poem by Joseph Rodman Drake see page 94.

While memory bids me weep thee,
    Nor thoughts nor words are free,—
The grief is fixed too deeply
    That mourns a man like thee.

JOHN HOWARD PAYNE

(*1791-1852*)

Home, Sweet Home

Mid pleasures and palaces though we may roam,
Be it ever so humble, there's no place like home;
A charm from the sky seems to hallow us there,
Which, seek through the world, is ne'er met with elsewhere.
Home, Home, sweet Home!
There's no place like Home! there's no place like Home!

An exile from home, splendor dazzles in vain;
O, give me my lowly thatched cottage again!
The birds singing gayly, that came at my call,
Give me them, and the peace of mind, dearer than all!
Home, Home, sweet Home!
There's no place like Home! there's no place like Home!

How sweet 'tis to sit 'neath a fond father's smile,
And the cares of a mother to soothe and beguile!
Let others delight mid new pleasures to roam,
But give me, oh give me, the pleasures of home!
Home! Home! sweet Home!
There's no place like Home! there's no place like Home!

To thee I'll return, overburdened with care;
The heart's dearest solace will smile on me there;
No more from that cottage again will I roam;
Be it ever so humble, there's no place like home.
Home! Home! sweet Home!
There's no place like Home! there's no place like Home!

WILLIAM CULLEN BRYANT

(*1794-1878*)

To a Waterfowl

Whither, 'midst falling dew,
While glow the heavens with the last steps of day,
Far, through their rosy depths, dost thou pursue
    Thy solitary way!

Vainly the fowler's eye
Might mark thy distant flight to do thee wrong,
As, darkly painted on the crimson sky,
    Thy figure floats along.

Seek'st thou the plashy brink
Of weedy lake, or marge of river wide,
Or where the rocking billows rise and sink
    On the chafed ocean side?

There is a Power whose care
Teaches thy way along that pathless coast—
The desert and illimitable air—
    Lone wandering, but not lost.

All day thy wings have fanned,
At that far height, the cold, thin atmosphere;
Yet stoop not, weary, to the welcome land,
    Though the dark night is near.

And soon that toil shall end;
Soon shalt thou find a summer home, and rest
And scream among thy fellows; reeds shall bend
    Soon o'er thy sheltered nest.

Thou'rt gone; the abyss of heaven
Hath swallowed up thy form; yet on my heart
Deeply hath sunk the lesson thou hast given,
    And shall not soon depart.

He, who, from zone to zone,
Guides through the boundless sky thy certain flight,
In the long way that I must tread alone,
    Will lead my steps aright.

Thanatopsis

To him who in the love of Nature holds
Communion with her visible forms, she speaks
A various language; for his gayer hours
She has a voice of gladness, and a smile
And eloquence of beauty, and she glides
Into his darker musings, with a mild
And healing sympathy, that steals away
Their sharpness, ere he is aware. When thoughts
Of the last bitter hour come like a blight
Over thy spirit, and sad images
Of the stern agony, and shroud, and pall,
And breathless darkness, and the narrow house,
Make thee to shudder, and grow sick at heart;—
Go forth, under the open sky, and list

To Nature's teachings, while from all around—
Earth and her waters, and the depths of air,—
Comes a still voice—Yet a few days, and thee
The all-beholding sun shall see no more
In all his course; nor yet in the cold ground,
Where thy pale form was laid with many tears,
Nor in the embrace of ocean, shall exist
Thy image. Earth, that nourished thee, shall claim
Thy growth, to be resolved to earth again,
And, lost each human trace, surrendering up
Thine individual being, shalt thou go
To mix forever with the elements,
To be a brother to the insensible rock
And to the sluggish clod, which the rude swain
Turns with his share, and treads upon. The oak
Shall send his roots abroad, and pierce thy mould.

Yet not to thine eternal resting-place
Shalt thou retire alone—nor couldst thou wish
Couch more magnificent. Thou shalt lie down
With patriarchs of the infant world—with kings,
The powerful of the earth—the wise, the good.
Fair forms, and hoary seers of ages past,
All in one mighty sepulchre.—The hills
Rock-ribbed and ancient as the sun,—the vales
Stretching in pensive quietness between;
The venerable woods—rivers that move
In majesty, and the complaining brooks
That make the meadows green; and, poured round all,
Old ocean's gray and melancholy waste,—
Are but the solemn decorations all
Of the great tomb of man. The golden sun,

The planets, all the infinite host of heaven,
Are shining on the sad abodes of death,
Through the still lapse of ages. All that tread
The globe are but a handful to the tribes
That slumber in its bosom.—Take the wings
Of morning—and the Barcan desert pierce,
Or lose thyself in the continuous woods
Where rolls the Oregon, and hears no sound,
Save his own dashings—yet—the dead are there;
And millions in those solitudes, since first
The flight of years began, have laid them down
In their last sleep—the dead reign there alone.
So shalt thou rest—and what if thou withdraw
Unheeded by the living—and no friend
Take note of thy departure? All that breathe
Will share thy destiny. The gay will laugh
When thou art gone, the solemn brood of care
Plod on, and each one as before will chase
His favorite phantom; yet all these shall leave
Their mirth and their employments, and shall come,
And make their bed with thee. As the long train
Of ages glide away, the sons of men,
The youth in life's green spring, and he who goes
In the full strength of years, matron, and maid,
And the sweet babe, and the gray-headed man,—
Shall one by one be gathered to thy side,
By those, who in their turn shall follow them.

So live, that when thy summons comes to join
The innumerable caravan, that moves
To that mysterious realm, where each shall take
His chamber in the silent halls of death,

Thou go not, like the quarry-slave at night,
Scourged to his dungeon, but, sustained and soothed
By an unfaltering trust, approach thy grave,
Like one who wraps the drapery of his couch
About him, and lies down to pleasant dreams.

To the Fringed Gentian

Thou blossom bright with autumn dew,
And colored with the heaven's own blue,
That openest, when the quiet light
Succeeds the keen and frosty night.

Thou comest not when violets lean
O'er wandering brooks and springs unseen,
Or columbines, in purple dressed,
Nod o'er the ground-bird's hidden nest.

Thou waitest late, and com'st alone,
When woods are bare and birds are flown,
And frosts and shortening days portend
The aged year is near his end.

Then doth thy sweet and quiet eye
Look through its fringes to the sky
Blue—blue—as if that sky let fall
A flower from its cerulean wall.

I would that thus, when I shall see
The hour of death draw near to me,
Hope, blossoming within my heart,
May look to heaven as I depart.

85

The Yellow Violet

When beechen buds begin to swell,
  And woods the blue-birds warble know,
The yellow violet's modest bell
  Peeps from the last year's leaves below.

Ere russet fields their green resume,
  Sweet flower, I love, in forest bare,
To meet thee, when thy faint perfume
  Alone is in the virgin air.

Of all her train, the hands of Spring
  First plant thee in the watery mould,
And I have seen thee blossoming
  Beside the snow-bank's edges cold.

Thy parent sun, who bade thee view
  Pale skies, and chilling moisture sip,
Has bathed thee in his own bright hue,
  And streaked with jet thy glowing lip.

Yet slight thy form, and low thy seat,
  And earthward bent thy gentle eye,
Unapt the passing view to meet,
  When loftier flowers are flaunting nigh.

Oft, in the sunless April day,
  Thy early smile has stayed my walk,
But midst the gorgeous blooms of May,
  I passed thee on thy humble stalk.

So they, who climb to wealth, forget
   The friends in darker fortunes tried.
I copied them—but I regret
   That I should ape the ways of pride

And when again the genial hour
   Awakes the painted tribes of light,
I'll not o'erlook the modest flower
   That made the woods of April bright.

Song of Marion's Men

Our band is few, but true and tried,
   Our leader frank and bold;
The British soldier trembles
   When Marion's name is told.
Our fortress is the good green wood,
   Our tent the cypress-tree;
We know the forest round us,
   As seamen know the sea.
We know its walls of thorny vines
   Its glades of reedy grass,
Its safe and silent islands
   Within the dark morass.

Woe to the English soldiery
   That little dread us near!
On them shall light at midnight
   A strange and sudden fear:
When waking to their tents on fire
   They grasp their arms in vain,

And they who stand to face us
   Are beat to earth again;
And they who fly in terror deem
   A mighty host behind,
And hear the tramp of thousands
   Upon the hollow wind.

Then sweet the hour that brings release
   From danger and from toil:
We talk the battle over,
   And share the battle's spoil.
The woodland rings with laugh and shout,
   As if a hunt were up,
And woodland flowers are gathered
   To crown the soldier's cup.
With merry songs we mock the wind
   That in the pine-top grieves,
And slumber long and sweetly,
   On beds of oaken leaves.

Well knows the fair and friendly moon
   The band that Marion leads—
The glitter of their rifles,
   The scampering of their steeds.
'Tis life our fiery barbs to guide
   Across the moonlight plains;
'Tis life to feel the night-wind
   That lifts their tossing names.
A moment in the British camp—
   A moment—and away
Back to the pathless forest,
   Before the peep of day.

Grave men there are by broad Santee
  Grave men with hoary hairs,
Their hearts are all with Marion,
  For Marion are their prayers.
And lovely ladies greet our band,
  With kindliest welcoming,
With smiles like those of summer,
  And tears like those of spring.
For them we wear these trusty arms,
  And lay them down no more
Till we have driven the Briton,
  Forever, from our shore.

America

O mother of a mighty race,
Yet lovely in thy youthful grace!
The elder dames, thy haughty peers,
Admire and hate thy blooming years;
    With words of shame
And taunts of scorn they join thy name.

For on thy cheeks the glow is spread
That tints thy morning hills with red;
Thy step,—the wild deer's rustling feet
Within thy woods are not more fleet;
    Thy hopeful eye
Is bright as thine own sunny sky.

Ay, let them rail, those haughty ones,
While safe thou dwellest with thy sons.

They do not know how loved thou art,
How many a fond and fearless heart
      Would rise to throw
Its life between thee and the foe.

They know not, in their hate and pride,
What virtues with thy children bide,—
How true, how good, thy graceful maids
Make bright, like flowers, the valley shades;
      What generous men
Spring, like thine oaks, by hill and glen;

What cordial welcomes greet the guest
By thy lone rivers of the west;
How faith is kept, and truth revered,
And man is loved, and God is feared,
      In woodland homes,
And where the ocean border foams.

There's freedom at thy gates, and rest
For earth's down-trodden and opprest,
A shelter for the hunted head,
For the starved laborer toil and bread.
      Power, at thy bounds,
Stops, and calls back his baffled hounds.

O fair young mother! on thy brow
Shall sit a nobler grace than now.
Deep in the brightness of thy skies,
The thronging years in glory rise,
      And, as thy fleet,
Drop strength and riches at thy feet.

Thine eye, with every coming hour,
Shall brighten, and thy form shall tower;
And when thy sisters, elder born,
Would brand thy name with words of scorn,
     Before thine eye
Upon their lips the taunt shall die.

The Death of Lincoln

Oh, slow to smite and swift to spare,
   Gentle and merciful and just!
Who, in the fear of God, didst bear
   The sword of power, a nation's trust!

In sorrow by thy bier we stand,
   Amid the awe that hushes all,
And speak the anguish of a land
   That shook with horror at thy fall.

Thy task is done; the bond are free:
   We bear thee to an honored grave,
Whose proudest monument shall be
   The broken fetters of the slave.

Pure was thy life; its bloody close
   Hath placed thee with the sons of light,
Among the noble host of those
   Who perished in the cause of Right.

From "*The Antiquity of Freedom*"

Oh Freedom! thou art not, as poets dream,
A fair young girl, with light and delicate limbs,
And wavy tresses gushing from the cap
With which the Roman master crowned his slave
When he took off the gyves. A bearded man,
Armed to the teeth, art thou; one mailed hand
Grasps the broad shield, and one the sword; thy brow,
Glorious in beauty though it be, is scarred
With tokens of old wars; thy massive limbs
Are strong with struggling. Power at thee has launched
His bolts, and with his lightnings smitten thee;
They could not quench the life thou hast from heaven.
Merciless power has dug thy dungeon deep,
And his swart armorers, by a thousand fires,
Have forged thy chain; yet, while he deems thee bound,
The links are shivered, and the prison walls
Fall outward: terribly thou springest forth,
As springs the flame above a burning pile,
And shoutest to the nations, who return
Thy shoutings, while the pale oppressor flies.

Thy birthright was not given by human hands:
Thou wert twin-born with Man. In pleasant fields,
While yet our race was few, thou sat'st with him,
To tend the quiet flock and watch the stars,
And teach the reed to utter simple airs.
Thou by his side, amid the tangled wood,
Didst war upon the panther and the wolf,

His only foes; and thou with him didst draw
The earliest furrows on the mountain side,
Soft with the deluge. . . . Oh! not yet
May'st thou unbrace thy corslet, nor lay by
Thy sword. Nor yet, O Freedom, close thy lids
In slumber. For thine enemy never sleeps,
And thou must watch and combat till the day
Of the new earth and heaven.

JOSEPH RODMAN DRAKE

(*1795-1820*)

The American Flag

I

When Freedom from her mountain height
  Unfurl'd her standard to the air,
She tore the azure robe of night,
  And set the stars of glory there.
She mingled with its gorgeous dyes
The milky baldric of the skies,
And striped its pure celestial white
With streakings of the morning light;
Then from his mansion in the sun
She call'd her eagle bearer down,
And gave into his mighty hand
The symbol of her chosen land.

II

Majestic monarch of the cloud,
  Who rear'st aloft thy regal form,
To hear the tempest trumpings loud
And see the lightning lances driven,
  When strive the warriors of the storm,
And rolls the thunder-drum of heaven,
Child of the sun! to thee 'tis given
  To guard the banner of the free,
To hover in the sulphur smoke,
To ward away the battle stroke,

And bid its blendings shine afar,
Like rainbows on the cloud of war,
  The harbingers of victory!

III

Flag of the brave! thy folds shall fly,
  The sign of hope and triumph high,
When speaks the signal trumpet tone,
  And the long line comes gleaming on.
Ere yet the life-blood, warm and wet,
  Has dimm'd the glistening bayonet,
Each soldier eye shall brightly turn
  To where thy sky-born glories burn;
And, as his springing steps advance,
Catch war and vengeance from the glance.
And when the cannon-mouthings loud
  Heave in wild wreaths the battle-shroud
And gory sabres rise and fall
Like shoots of flame on midnight's pall;
  Then shall thy meteor glances glow,
And cowering foes shall shrink beneath
  Each gallant arm that strikes below
That lovely messenger of death.

IV

Flag of the seas! on ocean wave
Thy stars shall glitter o'er the brave;
When death, careering on the gale,
Sweeps darkly round the bellied sail,
And freighted waves rush wildly back
Before the broadside's reeling rack,
Each dying wanderer of the sea

Shall look at once to heaven and thee,
And smile to see thy splendour fly
In triumph o'er his closing eye.

v

Flag of the free heart's hope and home!
  By angel hands to valor given;
The stars have lit the welkin dome,
  And all thy hues were born in heaven.
Forever float that standard sheet!
  Where breathes the foe but falls before us,
With Freedom's soil beneath our feet,
  And Freedom's banner streaming o'er us!

JAMES GATES PERCIVAL

(*1795-1856*)

Seneca Lake

On thy fair bosom, silver lake,
   The wild swan spreads his snowy sail,
And round his breast the ripples break,
   As down he bears before the gale.

On thy fair bosom, waveless stream,
   The dipping paddle echoes far,
And flashes in the moonlight gleam,
   And bright reflects the polar star.

The waves along thy pebbly shore,
   As blows the north wind, heave their foam,
And curl around the dashing oar,
   As late the boatman hies him home.

How sweet, at set of sun, to view
   Thy golden mirror spreading wide,
And see the mist of mantling blue
   Float round the distant mountain's side!

At midnight hour, as shines the moon,
   A sheet of silver spreads below,
And swift she cuts, at highest noon,
   Light clouds, like wreaths of purest snow.

On thy fair bosom, silver lake,
  O! I could ever sweep the oar,
When early birds at morning wake,
  And evening tells us toil is o'er.

GEORGE HILL

(*1796-1871*)

Leila

When first you look upon her face,
  You little note beside
The timidness that still betrays
  The beauties it would hide:
But one by one, they look out from
  Her blushes and her eyes;
And still the last the loveliest,
  Like stars from twilight skies.

And thoughts go sporting through her mind,
  Like children among flowers;
And deeds of gentle goodness are
  The measure of her hours.
In soul or face, she bears no trace
  Of one from Eden driven,
But, like the rainbow, seems, though born
  Of earth, a part of heaven.

EDWARD COOTE PINKNEY

(*1802-1828*)

Serenade

Look out upon the stars, my love,
    And shame them with thine eyes,
On which, than on the lights above,
    There hang more destinies.
Night's beauty is the harmony
    Of blending shades and light;
Then, lady, up,—look out, and be
    A sister to the night!

Sleep not! thine image wakes for aye
    Within my watching breast:
Sleep not! from her soft sleep should fly
    Who robs all hearts of rest.
Nay, lady, from thy slumbers break,
    And make this darkness gay
With looks, whose brightness well might make
    Of darker nights a day.

A Health

I fill this cup to one made up
    Of loveliness alone,
A woman, of her gentle sex
    The seeming paragon;

To whom the better elements
  And kindly stars have given
A form so fair, that, like the air,
  'T is less of earth than heaven.

Her every tone is music's own,
  Like those of morning birds,
And something more than melody
  Dwells ever in her words;
The coinage of her heart are they,
  And from her lips each flows,
As one may see the burdened bee
  Forth issue from the rose.

Affections are as thoughts to her,
  The measures of her hours;
Her feelings have the fragrancy,
  The freshness of young flowers;
And lovely passions, changing oft,
  So fill her, she appears
The image of themselves by turns,—
  The idol of past years!

Of her bright face one glance will trace
  A picture on the brain,
And of her voice in echoing hearts
  A sound must long remain;
But memory, such as mine of her,
  So very much endears,
When death is nigh my latest sigh
  Will not be life's, but hers.

I fill this cup to one made up
  Of loveliness alone,
A woman, of her gentle sex
  The seeming paragon.
Her health! and would on earth there stood
  Some more of such a frame,
That life might be all poetry,
  And weariness a name.

GEORGE POPE MORRIS

(*1802-1864*)

Woodman, Spare That Tree

Woodman, spare that tree!
  Touch not a single bough!
In youth it sheltered me,
  And I'll protect it now.
'Twas my forefather's hand
  That placed it near his cot;
There, woodman, let it stand,
  Thy axe shall harm it not.

That old familiar tree,
  Whose glory and renown
Are spread o'er land and sea—
  And wouldst thou hew it down?
Woodman, forbear thy stroke!
  Cut not its earth-bound ties;
Oh, spare that aged oak
  Now towering to the skies!

When but an idle boy,
  I sought its grateful shade;
In all their gushing joy
  Here, too, my sisters played.
My mother kissed me here;
  My father pressed my hand—
Forgive this foolish tear,
  But let that old oak stand.

My heart-strings round thee cling,
  Close as thy bark, old friend!
Here shall the wild-bird sing,
  And still thy branches bend.
Old tree, the storm still brave!
  And, woodman, leave the spot;
While I've a hand to save,
  Thy axe shall harm it not.

RALPH WALDO EMERSON

(1803-1882)

Hymn

(Sung at the Completion of the Concord Monument,
April 19, 1836)

By the rude bridge that arched the flood,
    Their flag to April's breeze unfurled,
Here once the embattled farmers stood,
    And fired the shot heard round the world.

The foe long since in silence slept;
    Alike the conqueror silent sleeps;
And Time the ruined bridge has swept
    Down the dark stream which seaward creeps.

On this green bank, by this soft stream,
    We set today a votive stone;
That memory may their deed redeem,
    When, like our sires, our sons are gone.

Spirit, that made those heroes dare
    To die, or leave their children free,
Bid Time and Nature gently spare
    The shaft we raise to them and thee.

The Rhodora

On Being Asked, Whence Is the Flower?

In May, when sea-winds pierced our solitudes,
I found the fresh Rhodora in the woods,
Spreading its leafless blooms in a damp nook,
To please the desert and the sluggish brook.
The purple petals, fallen in the pool,
Made the black water with their beauty gay;
Here might the red-bird come his plumes to cool,
And court the flower that cheapens his array.
Rhodora! if the sages ask thee why
This charm is wasted on the earth and sky,
Tell them, dear, that if eyes were made for seeing,
Then Beauty is its own excuse for being:
Why thou wert there, O rival of the rose!
I never thought to ask, I never knew;
But, in my simple ignorance, suppose
The self-same Power that brought me there brought you.

Forebearance

Hast thou named all the birds without a gun?
Loved the wood-rose, and left it on its stalk?
At rich men's tables eaten bread and pulse?
Unarmed, faced danger with a heart of trust?
And loved so well a high behaviour,
In man or maid, that thou from speech refrained,
Nobility more nobly to repay?
O, be my friend, and teach me to be thine!

The Snow-Storm

Announced by all the trumpets of the sky,
Arrives the snow, and, driving o'er the fields,
Seems nowhere to alight: the whited air
Hides hills and woods, the river, and the heaven,
And veils the farm-house at the garden's end.
The sled and traveller stopped, the courier's feet
Delayed, all friends shut out, the housemates sit
Around the radiant fireplace, enclosed
In a tumultuous privacy of storm.

Come see the north wind's masonry.
Out of an unseen quarry evermore
Furnished with tile, the fierce artificer
Curves his white bastions with projected roof
Round every windward stake, or tree, or door.
Speeding, the myriad-handed, his wild work
So fanciful, so savage, nought cares he
For number or proportion. Mockingly,
On coop or kennel he hangs Parian wreaths;
A swan-like form invests the hidden thorn;
Fills up the farmer's lane from wall to wall,
Maugre the farmer's sighs; and, at the gate,
A tapering turret overtops the work.
And when his hours are numbered, and the world
Is all his own, retiring, as he were not,
Leaves, when the sun appears, astonished Art
To mimic in slow structures, stone by stone,
Built in an age, the mad wind's night-work,
The frolic architecture of the snow.

Fate

Deep in the man sits fast his fate
To mould his fortunes mean or great:
Unknown to Cromwell as to me
Was Cromwell's measure or degree;
Unknown to him, as to his horse,
If he than his groom be better or worse.
He works, plots, fights, in rude affairs,
With squires, lords, kings, his craft compares,
Till late he learned, through doubt and fear,
Broad England harboured not his peer:
Obeying Time, the last to own
The Genius from its cloudy throne.
For the prevision is allied
Unto the thing so signified;
Or say, the foresight that awaits
Is the same Genius that creates.

Good-bye

Good-bye, proud world! I'm going home:
Thou art not my friend, and I'm not thine.
Long through thy weary crowds I roam;
A river-ark on the ocean brine,
Long I've been tossed like the driven foam;
But now, proud world! I'm going home.
Good-bye to Flattery's fawning face;
To Grandeur with his wise grimace;

To upstart Wealth's averted eye;
To supple Office, low and high;
To crowded halls, to court and street;
To frozen hearts and hasting feet;
To those who go, and those who come;
Good-bye, proud world! I'm going home.

I am going to my own hearth-stone,
Bosomed in yon green hills alone,—
A secret nook in a pleasant land,
Whose groves the frolic fairies planned;
Where arches green, the livelong day,
Echo the blackbird's roundelay,
And vulgar feet have never trod
A spot that is sacred to thought and God.

O, when I am safe in my sylvan home,
I tread on the pride of Greece and Rome;
And when I am stretched beneath the pines,
Where the evening star so holy shines,
I laugh at the lore and the pride of man,
At the sophist schools, and the learned clan;
For what are they all, in their high conceit,
When man in the bush with God may meet?

The Hero

Ruby Wine is drunk by knaves,
Sugar spends to fatten slaves,
Rose and vine-leaf deck buffoons;
Thunder-clouds are Jove's festoons,

109

Drooping oft in wreaths of dread,
Lightning knotted round his head;
The hero is not fed on sweets,
Daily his own heart he eats;
Chambers of the great are jails,
And head-winds right for royal sails.

Mithridates

I cannot spare water or wine,
    Tobacco-leaf, or poppy, or rose;
From the earth-poles to the Line,
    All between that works or grows,
Every thing is kin of mine.

Give me agates for my meat;
Give me cantharids to eat;
From air and ocean bring me foods,
From all zones and altitudes;—

From all natures, sharp and slimy,
    Salt and basalt, wild and tame:
Tree and lichen, ape, sea-lion,
    Bird, and reptile, be my game.

Ivy for my fillet band;
Blinding dog-wood in my hand;
Hemlock for my sherbet cull me,
And the prussic juice to lull me;
Swing me in the upas boughs,
Vampyre-fanned, when I carouse.

Too long shut in strait and few,
Thinly dieted on dew,
I will use the world, and sift it,
To a thousand humors shift it,
As you spin a cherry.
O doleful ghosts, and goblins merry!
O all you virtues, methods, mights,
Means, appliances, delights,
Reputed wrongs and braggart rights,
Smug routine, and things allowed,
Minorities, things under cloud!
Hither, take me, use me, fill me,
Vein and artery, though ye kill me!

Two Rivers

Thy summer voice, Musketaquit,
Repeats the music of the rain;
But sweeter rivers pulsing flit
Through thee, as thou through Concord Plain.

Thou in thy narrow banks art pent:
The stream I love unbounded goes
Through flood and sea and firmament;
Through light, through life, it forward flows.

I see the inundation sweet,
I hear the spending of the stream
Through years, through men, through Nature fleet,
Through love and thought, through power and dream.

Musketaquit, a goblin strong,
Of shard and flint makes jewels gay;
They lose their grief who hear his song,
And where he winds is the day of day.

So forth and brighter fares my stream,—
Who drink it shall not thirst again;
No darkness stains its equal gleam
And ages drop in it like rain.

Wealth

Who shall tell what did befall,
Far away in time, when once,
Over the lifeless ball,
Hung idle stars and suns?
What god the element obeyed?
Wings of what wind the lichen bore,
Wafting the puny seeds of power,
Which, lodged in rock, the rock abrade?
And well the primal pioneer
Knew the strong task to it assigned,
Patient through Heaven's enormous year
To build in matter home for mind.
From air the creeping centuries drew
The matted thicket low and wide,
This must the leaves of ages strew
The granite slab to clothe and hide,
Ere wheat can wave its golden pride.
What smiths, and in what furnace, rolled
(In dizzy aeons dim and mute

The reeling brain can ill compute)
Copper and iron, lead and gold?
What oldest star the fame can save
Of races perishing to pave
The planet with a floor of lime?
Dust is their pyramid and mole:
Who saw what ferns and palms were pressed
Under the tumbling mountain's breast,
In the safe herbal of the coal?
But when the quarried means were piled,
All is waste and worthless, till
Arrives the wise selecting will,
And, out of slime and chaos, Wit
Draws the threads of fair and fit.
Then temples rose, and towns, and marts,
The shop of toil, the hall of arts;
Then flew the sail across the seas
To feed the North from tropic trees;
The storm-wind wove, the torrent span,
Where they were bid the rivers ran;
New slaves fulfilled the poet's dream,
Galvanic wire, strong-shouldered steam.
Then docks were built, and crops were stored,
And ingots added to the hoard.
But, though light-headed man forget,
Remembering Matter pays her debt:
Still, though her motes and masses, draw
Electric thrills and ties of Law,
Which bind the strength of Nature wild
To the conscience of a child.

Days

Daughters of Time, the hypocritic Days,
Muffled and dumb like barefoot dervishes,
And marching single in an endless file,
Bring diadems and fagots in their hands.
To each they offer gifts after his will,
Bread, kingdoms, stars, and sky that holds them all.
I, in my pleached garden, watched the pomp,
Forgot my morning wishes, hastily
Took a few herbs and apples, and the Day
Turned and departed silent. I, too late,
Under her solemn fillet saw the scorn.

The Apology

Think me not unkind and rude
    That I walk alone in grove and glen;
I go to the god of the wood
    To fetch his word to men.

Tax not my sloth that I
    Fold my arms beside the brook;
Each cloud that floated in the sky
    Writes a letter in my book.

Chide me not, laborious band,
    For the idle flowers I brought;
Every aster in my hand
    Goes home loaded with a thought.

There was never mystery
   But 'tis figured in the flowers;
Was never secret history
   But birds tell it in the bowers.

One harvest from thy field
   Homeward brought the oxen strong;
A second crop thine acres yield,
   Which I gather in a song.

Bacchus

Bring me wine, but wine which never grew
In the belly of the grape,
Or grew on vine whose tap-roots, reaching through
Under the Andes to the Cape,
Suffered no savour of the earth to scape.

Let its grapes the morn salute
From a nocturnal root,
Which feels the acrid juice
Of Styx and Erebus;
And turns the woe of Night,
By its own craft, to a more rich delight.

We buy ashes for bread;
We buy diluted wine;
Give me of the true,—
Whose ample leaves and tendrils curled
Among the silver hills of heaven,
Draw everlasting dew;

Wine of wine,
Blood of the world,
Form of forms, and mould of statures,
That I intoxicated,
And by the draught assimilated,
May float at pleasure through all natures;
The bird-language rightly spell,
And that which roses say so well.
Wine that is shed
Like the torrents of the sun
Up the horizon walls,
Or like the Atlantic streams, which run
When the South Sea calls.

Water and bread,
Food which needs no transmuting,
Rainbow-flowering, wisdom-fruiting
Wine which is already man,
Food which teach and reason can.

Wine which Music is,—
Music and wine are one,—
That I, drinking this,
Shall hear far Chaos talk with me;
Kings unborn shall walk with me;
And the poor grass shall plot and plan
What it will do when it is man.
Quickened so, will I unlock
Every crypt of every rock.

I thank the joyful juice
For all I know;—

Winds of remembering
Of the ancient being blow,
And seeming-solid walls of use
Open and flow.

Pour, Bacchus! the remembering wine;
Retrieve the loss of me and mine!
Vine for vine be antidote,
And the grape requite the lote!
Haste to cure the old despair,—
Reason in Nature's lotus drenched,
The memory of ages quenched;
Give them again to shine;
Let wine repair what this undid;
And where the infection slid,
A dazzling memory revive;
Refresh the faded tints,
Recut the aged prints,
And write my old adventures with the pen
Which on the first day drew,
Upon the tablets blue,
The dancing Pleiads and eternal men.

Give All to Love

Give all to love;
Obey thy heart;
Friends, kindred, days,
Estate, good-fame,
Plans, credit, and the Muse,—
Nothing refuse.

'Tis a brave master;
Let it have scope:
Follow it utterly,
Hope beyond hope:
High and more high
It dives into noon,

With wing unspent,
Untold intent;
But it is a god,
Knows its own path,
And the outlets of the sky.

It was never for the mean;
It requireth courage stout,
Souls above doubt,
Valor unbending;
It will reward,—
They shall return
More than they were,
And ever ascending.

Leave all for love;
Yet, hear me, yet,
One word more thy heart behoved,
One pulse more of firm endeavor,—
Keep thee to-day
To-morrow, forever,
Free as an Arab
Of thy beloved.

Cling with life to the maid;
But when the surprise,
First vague shadow of surmise
Flits across her bosom young
Of a joy apart from thee,
Free be she, fancy-free;
Nor thou detain her vesture's hem,
Nor the palest rose she flung
From her summer diadem.

Though thou loved her as thyself,
As a self of purer clay,
Though her parting dims the day,
Stealing grace from all alive;
Heartily know,
When half-gods go,
The gods arrive.

Experience

The lords of life, the lords of life,—
I saw them pass,
In their own guise,
Like and unlike,
Portly and grim,—
Use and Surprise,
Surface and Dream,
Succession swift, and spectral Wrong,
Temperament without a tongue,
And the inventor of the game
Omnipresent without name;—

Some to see, some to be guessed,
They march from east to west:
Little man, least of all,
Among the legs of his guardians tall,
Walked about with puzzled look.
Him by the hand dear Nature took,
Dearest Nature, strong and kind,
Whispered, "Darling never mind!
Tomorrow they will wear another face,
The founder thou; these are thy race!"

Ode

Inscribed to W. H. Channing

Though loath to grieve
The evil time's sole patriot,
I cannot leave
My honeyed thought
For the priest's cant,
Or statesman's rant.

If I refuse
My study for their politique,
Which at the best is trick,
The angry Muse
Puts confusion in my brain.

But who is he that prates
Of the culture of mankind,
Of better arts and life?

Go, blindworm, go,
Behold the famous States
Harrying Mexico
With rifle and with knife!

Or who, with accent bolder,
Dare praise the freedom-loving mountaineer?
I found by thee, O rushing Contoocook!
And in thy valleys, Agiochook!
The jackals of the Negro-holder.

The God who made New Hampshire
Taunted the lofty land
With little men;—
Small bat and wren
House in the oak:—
If ear-fire cleave
The upheaved land, and bury the folk,
The Southern crocodile would grieve.

Virtue palters; Right is hence;
Freedom praised, but hid;
Funeral eloquence
Rattles the coffin-lid.

What boots thy zeal,
O glowing friend,
That would indignant rend
The Northland from the South?
Wherefore? to what good end?
Boston Bay and Bunker Hill
Would serve things still;—
Things are of the snake.

The horseman serves the horse,
The neatherd serves the neat,
The merchant serves the purse,
The eater serves his meat;
'Tis the day of the chattel,
Web to weave, and corn to grind;
Things are in the saddle,
And ride mankind.

There are two laws discrete,
Not reconciled,—
Law for man, and law for thing:
The last builds town and fleet,
But it runs wild,
And doth the man unking.

'Tis fit the forest fall,
The steep be graded,
The mountain tunnelled,
The sand shaded,
The orchard planted,
The glebe tilled,
The prairie granted,
The steamer built.

Let man serve law for man;
Live for friendship, live for love,
For truth's and harmony's behoof;
The state may follow how it can,
As Olympus follows Jove.

Yet do not I implore
The wrinkled shopman to my sounding woods,
Nor bid the unwilling senator
Ask votes of thrushes in the solitudes.
Every one to his chosen work;—
Foolish hands may mix and mar;
Wise and sure the issues are.
Round they roll till dark is light,
Sex to sex, and even to odd;—
The over-god
Who marries Right to Might,
Who peoples, unpeoples,—
He who exterminates
Races by stronger races,
Black by white faces,—
Knows to bring honey
Out of the lion;
Grafts gentlest scion
On pirate and Turk.

The Cossack eats Poland,
Like stolen fruit;
Her last noble is ruined,
Her last poet mute:
Straight, into double band
The victors divide;
Half for freedom strike and stand;—
The astonished Muse finds thousands at her side.

Uriel

It fell in the ancient periods
  Which the brooding soul surveys,
Or ever the wild Time coined itself
  Into calendar months and days.

This was the lapse of Uriel,
Which in Paradise befell.
Once, among the Pleiads walking,
Seyd overhead the young gods talking;
And the treason, too long pent,
To his ears was evident.
The young deities discussed
Laws of form, and metre just,
Orb, quintessence, and sunbeams,
What subsisteth, and what seems.
One, with low tones that decide,
And doubt and reverend use defied,
With a look that solved the sphere,
And stirred the devils everywhere,
Gave his sentiment divine
Against the being of a line.
'Line in nature is not found;
Unit and universe are round;
In vain produced, all rays return;
Evil will bless, and ice will burn.'
As Uriel spoke with piercing eye,
A shudder ran around the sky;
The stern old war-gods shook their heads,

The seraphs frowned from myrtle-beds;
Seemed to the holy festival
The rash word boded ill to all;
The balance-beam of Fate was bent;
The bounds of good and ill were rent;
Strong Hades could not keep his own,
But all slid to confusion.

A sad self-knowledge, withering, fell
On the beauty of Uriel;
In heaven once eminent, the god
Withdrew, that hour, into his cloud;
Whether doomed to long gyration
In the sea of generation,
Or by knowledge grown too bright
To hit the nerve of feebler sight.
Straightway, a forgetting wind
Stole over the celestial kind,
And their lips the secret kept,
If in aches the fire-seed slept.
But now and then, truth-speaking things
Shamed the angels' veiling wings;
And, shrilling from the solar course,
Or from fruit of chemic force,
Procession of a soul in matter,
Or the speeding change of water,
Or out of the good of evil born,
Came Uriel's voice of cherub scorn,
And a blush tinged the upper sky,
And the gods shook, they knew not why.

Music

Let me go where'er I will
I hear a sky-born music still:
It sounds from all things old,
It sounds from all things young;
From all that's fair, from all that's foul,
Peals out a cheerful song.

It is not only in the rose,
It is not only in the bird,
Not only where the rainbow blows,
Nor in the song of woman heard,
But in the darkest, meanest things
There alway, alway something sings.

'Tis not in the high stars alone,
Nor in the cup of budding flowers,
Nor in the redbreast's mellow tone,
Nor in the bow that smiles in showers,
But in the mud and scum of things
There alway, alway something sings.

Fable

The mountain and the squirrel
Had a quarrel;
And the former called the latter "Little Prig";
Bun replied,

"You are doubtless very big;
But all sorts of things and weather
Must be taken in together,
To make up a year
And a sphere.
And I think it no disgrace
To occupy my place.
If I'm not so large as you,
You are not so small as I,
And not half so spry.
I'll not deny you make
A very pretty squirrel track;
Talents differ; all is well and wisely put;
If I cannot carry forests on my back,
Neither can you crack a nut."

History

There is no great and no small
To the soul that maketh all:
And where it cometh, all things are;
And it cometh every where.

I am owner of the sphere,
Of the seven stars and the solar year,
Of Caesar's hand, and Plato's brain,
Of Lord Christ's heart, and Shakespeare's strain.

Brahma

If the red slayer think he slays,
　Or if the slain think he is slain,
They know not well the subtle ways
　I keep, and pass, and turn again.

Far or forgot to me is near;
　Shadow and sunlight are the same;
The vanquished gods to me appear;
　And one to me are shame and fame.

They reckon ill who leave me out;
　When me they fly, I am the wings;
I am the doubter and the doubt,
　And I the hymn the Brahmin sings.

The strong gods pine for my abode,
　And pine in vain the sacred Seven;
But thou, meek lover of the good!
　Find me, and turn thy back on heaven.

Terminus

It is time to be old,
To take in sail—
The god of bounds,
Who sets to seas a shore,
Came to me in his fatal rounds,

And said: "No more!
No farther spread
Thy broad ambitious branches, and thy root.
Fancy departs: no more invent,
Contract thy firmament
To compass of a tent.
There's not enough for this and that,
Make thy option which of two;
Economise the failing river,
Not the less revere the Giver,
Leave the many and hold the few.
Timely wise accept the terms,
Soften the fall with wary foot;
A little while
Still plan and smile,
And, fault of novel germs,
Mature the unfallen fruit.
Curse, if thou wilt, thy sires,
Bad husbands of their fires,
Who, when they gave thee breath,
Failed to bequeath
The needful sinew stark as once,
The Baresark marrow to thy bones,
But left a legacy of ebbing veins,
Inconstant heat and nerveless reins—
Amid the Muses, left thee deaf and dumb
Amid the gladiators, halt and numb."
As the bird trims her to the gale,
I trim myself to the storm of time,
I man the rudder, reef the sail,
Obey the voice at eve obeyed at prime:

"Lowly faithful, banish fear,
Right onward drive unarmed;
The port, well worth the cruise, is near,
And every wave is charmed."

HENRY WADSWORTH LONGFELLOW

(*1807-1882*)

The Arsenal at Springfield

This is the Arsenal. From floor to ceiling,
   Like a huge organ, rise the burnished arms;
But from their silent pipes no anthem pealing
   Startles the villages with strange alarms.

Ah! what a sound will rise, how wild and dreary,
   When the death-angel touches those swift keys!
What loud lament and dismal Miserere
   Will mingle with their awful symphonies!

I hear even now the infinite fierce chorus,
   The cries of agony, the endless groan,
Which, through the ages that have gone before us,
   In long reverberations reach our own.

On helm and harness rings the Saxon hammer,
   Through Cimbric forest roars the Norseman's song,
And loud, amid the universal clamor,
   O'er distant deserts sounds the Tartar gong.

I hear the Florentine, who from his palace
   Wheels out his battle-bell with dreadful din,
And Aztec priests upon their teocallis[1]
   Beat the wild war-drum made of serpent's skin;

[1] Flat-topped pyramids.

131

The tumult of each sacked and burning village:
    The shout that every prayer for mercy drowns;
The soldiers' revels in the midst of pillage;
    The wail of famine in beleaguered towns;

The bursting shell, the gateway wrenched asunder,
    The rattling musketry, the clashing blade;
And ever and anon, in tones of thunder,
    The diapason of the cannonade.

Is it, O man, with such discordant noises,
    With such accursed instruments as these,
Thou drownest Nature's sweet and kindly voices,
    And jarrest the celestial harmonies?

Were half the power, that fills the world with terror,
    Were half the wealth, bestowed on camps and courts,
Given to redeem the human mind from error,
    There were no need of arsenals nor forts:

The warrior's name would be a name abhorrèd!
    And every nation, that should lift again
Its hand against a brother, on its forehead
    Would wear forevermore the curse of Cain!

Down the dark future, through long generations,
    The echoing sounds grow fainter and then cease;
And like a bell, with solemn, sweet vibrations,
    I hear once more the voice of Christ say, "Peace!"

Peace! and no longer from its brazen portals
    The blast of War's great organ shakes the skies!

But beautiful as songs of the immortals,
  The holy melodies of love arise.

The Jewish Cemetery at Newport

How strange it seems! These Hebrews in their graves,
  Close by the street of this fair seaport town,
Silent beside the never-silent waves,
  At rest in all this moving up and down!

The trees are white with dust, that o'er their sleep
  Wave their broad curtains in the south-wind's breath,
While underneath such leafy tents they keep
  The long, mysterious Exodus of Death.

And these sepulchral stones, so old and brown,
  That pave with level flags their burial-place,
Seem like the tablets of the Law, thrown down
  And broken by Moses at the mountain's base.

The very names recorded here are strange,
  Of foreign accent, and of different climes;
Alvares and Rivera interchange
  With Abraham and Jacob of old times.

"Blessed be God! for he created Death!"
  The mourners said, "and Death is rest and peace";
Then added, in the certainty of faith,
  "And giveth Life that never more shall cease."

Closed are the portals of their Synagogue,
　No Psalms of David now the silence break,
No Rabbi reads the ancient Decalogue
　In the grand dialect the Prophets spake.

Gone are the living, but the dead remain,
　And not neglected; for a hand unseen,
Scattering its bounty, like a summer rain,
　Still keeps their graves and their remembrance green.

How came they here? What burst of Christian hate,
　What persecution, merciless and blind,
Drove o'er the sea—that desert desolate—
　These Ishmaels and Hagars of mankind?

They lived in narrow streets and lanes obscure,
　Ghetto and Judenstrass, in mirk and mire;
Taught in the school of patience to endure
　The life of anguish and the death of fire.

All their lives long, with the unleavened bread
　And bitter herbs of exile and its fears,
The wasting famine of the heart they fed,
　And slaked its thirst with marah of their tears.

Anathema maranatha! was the cry
　That ran from town to town, from street to street;
At every gate the accursed Mordecai
　Was mocked and jeered, and spurned by Christian feet.

Pride and humiliation hand in hand
　Walked with them through the world where'er they went;

134

Trampled and beaten were they as the sand,
  And yet unshaken as the continent.

For in the background figures vague and vast
  Of patriarchs and of prophets rose sublime,
And all the great traditions of the Past
  They saw reflected in the coming time.

And thus forever with reverted look
  The mystic volume of the world they read,
Spelling it backward, like a Hebrew book,
  Till life became a Legend of the Dead.

But ah! what once has been shall be no more!
  The groaning earth in travail and in pain
Brings forth its races, but does not restore,
  And the dead nations never rise again.

Nature

As a fond mother, when the day is o'er,
  Leads by the hand her little child to bed,
  Half willing, half reluctant to be led,
And leave his broken playthings on the floor,
Still gazing at them through the open door,
  Nor wholly reassured and comforted
  By promises of others in their stead,
Which, though more splendid, may not please him more;
So Nature deals with us, and takes away
  Our playthings one by one, and by the hand
  Leads us to rest so gently, that we go

135

Scarce knowing if we wish to go or stay,
   Being too full of sleep to understand
   How far the unknown transcends the what we know.

The Building of the Ship

"Build me straight, O worthy Master!
   Stanch and strong, a goodly vessel,
That shall laugh at all disaster,
   And with wave and whirlwind wrestle!"

The merchant's word
Delighted the Master heard;
For his heart was in his work, and the heart
Giveth grace unto every Art.
A quiet smile played round his lips,
As the eddies and dimples of the tide
Play round the bows of ships,
That steadily at anchor ride.
And with a voice that was full of glee,
He answered, "Ere long we will launch
A vessel as goodly, and strong, and stanch,
As ever weathered a wintry sea!"

And first with nicest skill and art,
Perfect and finished in every part,
A little model the Master wrought,
Which would be to the larger plan
What the child is to the man,
Its counterpart in miniature;

That with a hand more swift and sure
The greater labor might be brought
To answer to his inward thought.
And as he labored, his mind ran o'er
The various ships that were built of yore,
And above them all, and strangest of all,
Towered the Great Harry, crank and tall,
Whose picture was hanging on the wall,
With bows and stern raised high in air,
And balconies hanging here and there,
And signal lanterns and flags afloat,
And eight round towers, like those that frown
From some old castle, looking down
Upon the drawbridge and the moat.
And he said, with a smile, "Our ship, I wis,
Shall be of another form than this!"

It was of another form, indeed;
Built for freight, and yet for speed,
A beautiful and gallant craft;
Broad in the beam, that the stress of the blast,
Pressing down upon sail and mast,
Might not the sharp bows overwhelm;
Broad in the beam, but sloping aft
With graceful curve and slow degrees,
That she might be docile to the helm,
And that the currents of parted seas,
Closing behind, with mighty force,
Might aid and not impede her course.

In the ship-yard stood the Master,
  With the model of the vessel

That should laugh at all disaster,
    And with wave and whirlwind wrestle!

Covering many a rood of ground,
Lay the timber piled around;
Timber of chestnut, and elm, and oak,
And scattered here and there, with these,
The knarred and crooked cedar knees;
Brought from regions far away,
From Pascagoula's sunny bay,
And the banks of the roaring Roanoke!
Ah! what a wondrous thing it is
To note how many wheels of toil
One thought, one word, can set in motion!
There's not a ship that sails the ocean,
But every climate, every soil,
Must bring its tribute, great or small,
And help to build the wooden wall!

The sun was rising o'er the sea,
And long the level shadows lay,
As if they, too, the beams would be
Of some great, airy argosy,
Framed and launched in a single day.
That silent architect, the sun,
Had hewn and laid them every one,
Ere the work of man was yet begun.
Beside the Master, when he spoke,
A youth, against an anchor leaning,
Listened, to catch his slightest meaning.
Only the long waves, as they broke

In ripples on the pebbly beach,
Interrupted the old man's speech.

Beautiful they were, in sooth,
The old man and the fiery youth!
The old man, in whose busy brain
Many a ship that sailed the main
Was modeled o'er and o'er again;—
The fiery youth, who was to be
The heir of his dexterity,
The heir of his house, and his daughter's hand,
When he had built and launched from land
What the elder head had planned.
"Thus," said he, "will we build this ship!
Lay square the blocks upon the slip,
And follow well this plan of mine.
Choose the timbers with greatest care;
Of all that is unsound beware;
For only what is sound and strong
To this vessel shall belong.
Cedar of Maine and Georgia pine
Here together shall combine.
A goodly frame, and a goodly fame,
And the UNION be her name!
For the day that gives her to the sea
Shall give my daughter unto thee!"

The Master's word
Enraptured the young man heard;
And as he turned his face aside,
With a look of joy and a thrill of pride,
Standing before

Her father's door,
He saw the form of his promised bride.
The sun shone on her golden hair,
And her cheek was glowing fresh and fair,
With the breath of morn and the soft sea air,
Like a beauteous barge was she,
Still at rest on the sandy beach,
Just beyond the billow's reach;
But he
Was the restless, seething, stormy sea!

Ah, how skilful grows the hand
That obeyeth Love's command!
It is the heart, and not the brain,
That to the highest doth attain,
And he who followeth Love's behest
Far excelleth all the rest!

Thus with the rising of the sun
Was the noble task begun,
And soon throughout the ship-yard's bounds
Were heard the intermingled sounds
Of axes and of mallets, plied
With vigorous arms on every side;
Plied so deftly and so well,
That, ere the shadows of evening fell,
The keel of oak for a noble ship,
Scarfed and bolted, straight and strong,
Was lying ready, and stretched along
The blocks, well placed upon the slip.
Happy, thrice happy, every one
Who sees his labor well begun,

And not perplexed and multiplied,
By idly waiting for time and tide!
And when the hot, long day was o'er,
The young man at the Master's door
Sat with the maiden calm and still.
And, within the porch, a little more
Removed beyond the evening chill,
The father sat, and told them tales
Of wrecks in the great September gales,
Of pirates upon the Spanish Main,
And ships that never came back again,
The chance and change of a sailor's life,
Want and plenty, rest and strife,
His roving fancy, like the wind,
That nothing can stay and nothing can bind,
And the magic charm of foreign lands,
With shadows of palms, and shining sands,
Where the tumbling surf,
O'er the coral reefs of Madagascar,
Washes the feet of the swarthy Lascar,
As he lies alone and asleep on the turf.
And the trembling maiden held her breath
At the tales of that awful, pitiless sea,
With all its terror and mystery,
The dim, dark sea, so like unto Death,
That divides and yet unites mankind!
And whenever the old man paused, a gleam
From the bowl of his pipe would awhile illume
The silent group in the twilight gloom,
And thoughtful faces, as in a dream;
And for a moment one might mark
What had been hidden by the dark,

That the head of the maiden lay at rest,
Tenderly, on the young man's breast!

Day by day the vessel grew,
With timbers fashioned strong and true,
Stemson and keelson and sternson-knee,
Till, framed with perfect symmetry,
A skeleton ship rose up to view!
And around the bows and along the side
The heavy hammers and mallets plied,
Till after many a week, at length,
Wonderful for form and strength,
Sublime in its enormous bulk,
Loomed aloft the shadowy hulk!

And around it columns of smoke, upwreathing,
Rose from the boiling, bubbling, seething
Caldron, that glowed,
And overflowed
With the black tar, heated for the sheathing.
And amid the clamors
Of clattering hammers,
He who listened heard now and then
The song of the Master and his men:—
"Build me straight, O worthy Master,
    Stanch and strong, a goodly vessel,
That shall laugh at all disaster,
    And with wave and whirlwind wrestle!"

With oaken brace and copper band,
Lay the rudder on the sand,
That, like a thought, should have control

Over the movement of the whole;
And near it the anchor, whose giant hand
Would reach down and grapple with the land,
And immovable and fast
Hold the great ship against the bellowing blast!
And at the bows an image stood,
By a cunning artist carved in wood,
With robes of white, that far behind
Seemed to be fluttering in the wind.
It was not shaped in a classic mold,
Not like a nymph or Goddess of old,
Or naiad rising from the water,
But modeled from the Master's daughter!
On many a dreary and misty night,
'Twill be seen by the rays of the signal light,
Speeding along through the rain and the dark,
Like a ghost in its snow-white sark,
The pilot of some phantom bark,
Guiding the vessel, in its flight,
By a path none other knows aright!

Behold, at last,
Each tall and tapering mast
Is swung into its place;
Shrouds and stays
Holding it firm and fast!

Long ago,
In the deer-haunted forests of Maine,
When upon mountain and plain
Lay the snow,
They fell,—those lordly pines!

Those grand, majestic pines!
'Mid shouts and cheers
The jaded steers,
Panting beneath the goad,
Dragged down the weary, winding road
Those captive kings so straight and tall,
To be shorn of their streaming hair,
And, naked and bare,
To feel the stress and the strain
Of the wind and the reeling main,
Whose roar
Would remind them forevermore
Of their native forests they should not see again.

And everywhere
The slender, graceful spars
Poise aloft in the air,
And at the masthead,
White, blue, and red,
A flag unrolls the stripes and stars.
Ah! when the wanderer, lonely, friendless,
In foreign harbors shall behold
That flag unrolled,
'Twill be as a friendly hand
Stretched out from his native land,
Filling his heart with memories sweet and endless.

All is finished! and at length
Has come the bridal day
Of beauty and of strength.
Today the vessel shall be launched!
With fleecy clouds the sky is blanched,

And o'er the bay,
Slowly, in all his splendors dight,
The great sun rises to behold the sight.

The ocean old,
Centuries old,
Strong as youth, and as uncontrolled,
Paces restless to and fro,
Up and down the sands of gold.
His beating heart is not at rest;
And far and wide,
With ceaseless flow,
His beard of snow
Heaves with the heaving of his breast.

He waits impatient for his bride.
There she stands,
With her foot upon the sands,
Decked with flags and streamers gay,
In honor of her marriage day,
Her snow-white signals fluttering, blending,
Round her like a veil descending,
Ready to be
The bride of the gray, old sea.

On the deck another bride
Is standing by her lover's side.
Shadows from the flags and shrouds,
Like the shadows cast by clouds,
Broken by many a sunny fleck,
Fall around them on the deck.

The prayer is said,
The service read,
The joyous bridegroom bows his head;
And in tears the good old Master
Shakes the brown hand of his son,
Kisses his daughter's glowing cheek
In silence, for he cannot speak,
And ever faster
Down his own the tears begin to run.

The worthy pastor—
The shepherd of that wandering flock,
That has the ocean for its wold,
That has the vessel for its fold,
Leaping ever from rock to rock—
Spake, with accents mild and clear,
Words of warning, words of cheer,
But tedious to the bridegroom's ear.
He knew the chart
Of the sailor's heart,
All its pleasures and its griefs,
All its shallows and rocky reefs,
All those secret currents, that flow
With such resistless undertow,
And lift and drift, with terrible force,
The will from its moorings and its course.
Therefore he spake, and thus said he:—
"Like unto ships far off at sea,
Outward or homeward bound are we.
Before, behind, and all around,
Floats and swings the horizon's bound,
Seems at its distant rim to rise

And climb the crystal wall of the skies,
And then again to turn and sink,
As if we could slide from its outer brink.
Ah! it is not the sea,
It is not the sea that sinks and shelves,
But ourselves
That rock and rise
With endless and uneasy motion,
Now touching the very skies,
Now sinking into the depths of ocean.
Ah! if our souls but poise and swing
Like the compass in its brazen ring,
Ever level and ever true
To the toil and the task we have to do,
We shall sail securely, and safely reach
The Fortunate Isles, on whose shining beach
The sights we see, and the sounds we hear,
Will be those of joy and not of fear!"

Then the Master,
With a gesture of command,
Waved his hand;
And at the word,
Loud and sudden there was heard,
All around them and below,
The sound of hammers, blow on blow,
Knocking away the shores and spurs.
And see! she stirs!
She starts,—she moves,—she seems to feel
The thrill of life along her keel,
And, spurning with her foot the ground,
With one exulting, joyous bound,

She leaps into the ocean's arms!
And lo! from the assembled crowd
There rose a shout, prolonged and loud,
That to the ocean seemed to say,
"Take her, Oh bridegroom, old and gray,
Take her to thy protecting arms,
With all her youth and all her charms!"

How beautiful she is! How fair
She lies within those arms, that press
Her form with many a soft caress
Of tenderness and watchful care!
Sail forth into the sea, O ship!
Through wind and wave, right onward steer!
The moistened eye, the trembling lip,
Are not the signs of doubt or fear.

Sail forth into the sea of life,
O gentle, loving, trusting wife,
And safe from all adversity
Upon the bosom of that sea
Thy comings and thy goings be!
For gentleness and love and trust
Prevail o'er angry wave and gust;
And in the wreck of noble lives
Something immortal still survives!

Thou, too, sail on, O Ship of State!
Sail on, O Union, strong and great!
Humanity with all its fears,
With all the hopes of future years,
Is hanging breathless on thy fate!

We know what Master laid thy keel,
What Workmen wrought thy ribs of steel,
Who made each mast, and sail, and rope,
What anvils rang, what hammers beat,
In what a forge, and what a heat
Were shaped the anchors of thy hope!
Fear not each sudden sound and shock,
'Tis of the wave and not the rock;
'Tis but the flapping of the sail,
And not a rent made by the gale!
In spite of rock and tempest's roar,
In spite of false lights on the shore,
Sail on, nor fear to breast the sea!
Our hearts, our hopes, are all with thee,
Our hearts, our hopes, our prayers, our tears,
Our faith triumphant o'er our fears,
Are all with thee,—are all with thee!

The Arrow and the Song

I shot an arrow into the air,
It fell to earth, I knew not where;
For, so swiftly it flew, the sight
Could not follow it in its flight.

I breathed a song into the air,
It fell to earth, I knew not where;
For who has sight so keen and strong
That it can follow the flight of song?

149

Long, long afterward, in an oak
I found the arrow, still unbroke;
And the song, from beginning to end,
I found again in the heart of a friend.

A Psalm of Life

*What the Heart of the Young Man
Said to the Psalmist*

Tell me not, in mournful numbers,
    Life is but an empty dream!
For the soul is dead that slumbers,
    And things are not what they seem.

Life is real! Life is earnest!
    And the grave is not its goal;
Dust thou art, to dust returnest,
    Was not spoken of the soul.

Not enjoyment, and not sorrow,
    Is our destined end or way;
But to act, that each to-morrow
    Find us farther than to-day.

Art is long, and Time is fleeting,
    And our hearts, though stout and brave,
Still, like muffled drums, are beating
    Funeral marches to the grave.

In the world's broad field of battle,
  In the bivouac of Life,
Be not like dumb, driven cattle!
  Be a hero in the strife!

Trust no Future, howe'er pleasant!
  Let the dead Past bury its dead!
Act,—act in the living Present!
  Heart within, and God o'erhead!

Lives of great men all remind us
  We can make our lives sublime,
And, departing leave behind us
  Footprints on the sands of time;—

Footprints, that perhaps another,
  Sailing o'er life's solemn main,
A forlorn and shipwrecked brother,
  Seeing, shall take heart again.

Let us, then, be up and doing,
  With a heart for any fate;
Still achieving, still pursuing,
  Learn to labor and to wait.

The Rainy Day

The day is cold, and dark, and dreary;
It rains, and the wind is never weary;
The vine still clings to the mouldering wall,
But at every gust the dead leaves fall,
  And the day is dark and dreary.

My life is cold, and dark, and dreary;
It rains, and the wind is never weary;
My thoughts still cling to the mouldering Past,
But the hopes of youth fall thick in the blast,
    And the days are dark and dreary.

Be still, sad heart! and cease repining;
Behind the clouds is the sun still shining;
Thy fate is the common fate of all,
Into each life some rain must fall,
    Some days must be dark and dreary.

Hymn to the Night

I heard the trailing garments of the Night
    Sweep through her marble halls!
I saw her sable skirts all fringed with light
    From the celestial walls!

I felt her presence, by its spell of might,
    Stoop o'er me from above;
The calm, majestic presence of the Night,
    As of the one I love.

I heard the sounds of sorrow and delight,
    The manifold, soft chimes,
That fill the haunted chambers of the Night,
    Like some old poet's rhymes.

From the cool cisterns of the midnight air
    My spirit drank repose;

The fountain of perpetual peace flows there,—
    From those deep cisterns flows.

O holy Night! from thee I learn to bear
    What man has borne before!
Thou layest thy finger on the lips of Care,
    And they complain no more.

Peace! Peace! Orestes-like I breathe this prayer!
    Descend with broad-winged flight,
The welcome, the thrice-prayed-for, the most fair,
    The best-beloved Night!

Milton

I pace the sounding sea-beach and behold
How the voluminous billows roll and run,
Upheaving and subsiding, while the sun
Shines through their sheeted emerald far unrolled
And the ninth wave, slow gathering fold on fold
All its loose-flowing garments into one,
Plunges upon the shore, and floods the dun
Pale reach of sands, and changes them to gold.
So in majestic cadence rise and fall
The mighty undulations of thy song,
O sightless bard, England's Maeonides!
And ever and anon, high over all
Uplifted, a ninth wave superb and strong,
Floods all the soul with its melodious seas.

Chaucer

An old man in a lodge within a park;
The chamber walls depicted all around
With portraitures of huntsman, hawk, and hound,
And the hurt deer. He listeneth to the lark,
Whose song comes with the sunshine through the dark
Of painted glass in leaden lattice bound;
He listeneth and he laugheth at the sound,
Then writeth in a book like any clerk.
He is the poet of the dawn, who wrote
The Canterbury Tales, and his old age
Made beautiful with song; and as I read
I hear the crowing cock, I hear the note
Of lark and linnet, and from every page
Rise odors of plowed field or flowery mead.

The Village Blacksmith

Under a spreading chestnut-tree
   The village smithy stands;
The smith, a mighty man is he,
   With large and sinewy hands;
And the muscles of his brawny arms
   Are strong as iron bands.

His hair is crisp and black and long;
   His face is like the tan;
His brow is wet with honest sweat,—

He earns whate'er he can,
And looks the whole world in the face,
For he owes not any man.

Week in, week out, from morn till night,
You can hear his bellows blow;
You can hear him swing his heavy sledge,
With measured beat and slow,
Like a sexton ringing the village bell,
When the evening sun is low.

And children coming home from school,
Look in at the open door;
They love to see the flaming forge,
And hear the bellows roar,
And catch the burning sparks that fly
Like chaff from the threshing-floor.

He goes on Sunday to the church,
And sits among his boys;
He hears the parson pray and preach;
He hears his daughter's voice,
Singing in the village choir,
And it makes his heart rejoice.

It sounds to him like her mother's voice,
Singing in Paradise!
He needs must think of her once more,
How in the grave she lies;
And with his hard, rough hand he wipes
A tear out of his eyes.

Toiling, rejoicing, sorrowing,
  Onward through life he goes;
Each morning sees some task begin,
  Each evening sees it close;
Something attempted, something done,
  Has earned a night's repose.

Thanks, thanks to thee, my worthy friend,
  For the lesson thou hast taught!
Thus at the flaming forge of life
  Our fortunes must be wrought;
Thus on its sounding anvil shaped
  Each burning deed and thought!

The Tide Rises, the Tide Falls

The tide rises, the tide falls,
The twilight darkens, the curlew calls;
Along the sea-sands damp and brown
The traveller hastens toward the town,
  And the tide rises, the tide falls.

Darkness settles on roofs and walls,
But the sea, the sea in the darkness calls;
The little waves, with their soft, white hands,
Efface the footprints in the sands,
  And the tide rises, the tide falls.

The morning breaks; the steeds in their stalls
Stamp and neigh, as the hostler calls;

The day returns, but nevermore
Returns the traveller to the shore,
  And the tide rises, the tide falls.

My Lost Youth

Often I think of the beautiful town
  That is seated by the sea;
Often in thought go up and down
The pleasant streets of that dear old town,
  And my youth comes back to me.
    And a verse of a Lapland song
    Is haunting my memory still:
  "A boy's will is the wind's will,
And the thoughts of youth are long, long thoughts."

I can see the shadowy lines of its trees,
  And catch, in sudden gleams,
The sheen of the far-surrounding seas,
And islands that were the Hesperides
  Of all my boyish dreams.
    And the burden of that old song,
    It murmurs and whispers still:
  "A boy's will is the wind's will,
And the thoughts of youth are long, long thoughts."

I remember the black wharves and the slips,
  And the sea-tides tossing free:
And Spanish sailors with bearded lips,
And the beauty and mystery of the ships,
  And the magic of the sea. . . .

157

And the voice of that wayward song
Is singing and saying still:
"A boy's will is the wind's will,
And the thoughts of youth are long, long thoughts."

I remember the bulwarks by the shore,
And the fort upon the hill;
The sunrise gun, with its hollow roar,
The drum-beat repeated o'er and o'er,
And the bugle wild and shrill.
And the music of that old song
Throbs in my memory still:
"A boy's will is the wind's will,
And the thoughts of youth are long, long thoughts."

I remember the sea-fight far away,[1]
How it thundered o'er the tide!
And the dead captains, as they lay
In their graves, o'erlooking the tranquil bay,
Where they in battle died.
And the sound of that mournful song
Goes through me with a thrill:
"A boy's will is the wind's will,
And the thoughts of youth are long, long thoughts."

I can see the breezy dome of groves,
The shadows of Deering's Woods;
And the friendships old and the early loves
Come back with a Sabbath sound, as of doves
In quiet neighborhoods.

---

[1] Longfellow refers to the engagement between the *Enterprise* and *Boxer*, off the harbor of Portland, in which both captains were slain.

And the verse of that sweet old song,
  It flutters and murmurs still:
"A boy's will is the wind's will,
And the thoughts of youth are long, long thoughts."

I remember the gleams and glooms that dart
  Across the schoolboy's brain;
The song and the silence in the heart,
That in part are prophecies, and in part
  Are longings wild and vain.
    And the voice of that fitful song
    Sings on, and is never still:
"A boy's will is the wind's will,
And the thoughts of youth are long, long thoughts."

There are things of which I may not speak;
  There are dreams that cannot die;
There are thoughts that make the strong heart weak,
And bring a pallor into the cheek,
  And a mist before the eye.
    And the words of that fatal song
    Come over me like a chill:
"A boy's will is the wind's will,
And the thoughts of youth are long, long thoughts."

Strange to me now are the forms I meet
  When I visit the dear old town;
But the native air is pure and sweet,
And the trees that o'ershadow each well-known street,
  As they balance up and down,
    Are singing the beautiful song,
    Are sighing and whispering still:

"A boy's will is the wind's will,
And the thoughts of youth are long, long thoughts."

And Deering's Woods are fresh and fair,
  And with joy that is almost pain
My heart goes back to wander there,
And among the dreams of the days that were,
  I find my lost youth again.
    And the strange and beautiful song,
    The groves are repeating it still:
  "A boy's will is the wind's will,
And the thoughts of youth are long, long thoughts."

Snow-Flakes

Out of the bosom of the Air,
  Out of the cloud-folds of her garments shaken,
Over the woodlands brown and bare,
  Over the harvest-fields forsaken,
    Silent and soft and slow
    Descends the snow.

Even as our cloudy fancies take
  Suddenly shape in some divine expression,
Even as the troubled heart doth make
  In the white countenance confession,
    The troubled sky reveals
    The grief it feels.

This is the poem of the air,
Slowly in silent syllables recorded;
This is the secret of despair,
Long in its cloudy bosom hoarded,
Now whispered and revealed
To wood and field.

The Skeleton in Armor[1]

"Speak! speak! thou fearful guest!
Who, with thy hollow breast,
Still in rude armor drest,
Comest to daunt me!
Wrapt not in Eastern balms,
But with thy fleshless palms
Stretched, as if asking alms,
Why dost thou haunt me?"

Then from those cavernous eyes
Pale flashes seemed to rise,
As when the Northern skies
Gleam in December;
And, like the water's flow
Under December's snow,
Came a dull voice of woe
From the heart's chamber.

[1] "A skeleton had been dug up at Fall River clad in broken and corroded armor; and the idea occurred to me of connecting it with the Round Tower at Newport."—Longfellow's note.

"I was a Viking old!
My deeds, though manifold,
No Skald in song has told,
　No Saga taught thee!
Take heed that in thy verse
Thou dost the tale rehearse,
Else dread a dead man's curse;
　For this I sought thee.

"Far in the Northern Land,
By the wild Baltic's strand,
I, with my childish hand,
　Tamed the gerfalcon;
And, with my skates fast-found,
Skimmed the half-frozen Sound,
That the poor whimpering hound
　Trembled to walk on.

"Oft to his frozen lair
Tracked I the grisly bear,
While from my path the hare
　Fled like a shadow;
Oft through the forest dark
Followed the were-wolf's bark
Until the soaring lark
　Sang from the meadow.

"But when I older grew,
Joining a corsair's crew,
O'er the dark sea I flew
　With the marauders.

Wild was the life we led;
Many the souls that sped,
Many the hearts that bled,
  By our stern orders.

"Many a wassail-bout
Wore the long winter out;
Often our midnight shout
  Set the cocks crowing,
As we the Berserk's tale
Measured in cups of ale,
Draining the oaken pail
  Filled to o'erflowing.

"Once as I told in glee
Tales of the stormy sea,
Soft eyes did gaze on me,
  Burning yet tender;
And as the white stars shine
On the dark Norway pine,
On that dark heart of mine
  Fell their soft splendor.

"I wooed the blue-eyed maid,
Yielding, yet half afraid,
And in the forest's shade
  Our vows were plighted.
Under its loosened vest
Fluttered her little breast,
Like birds within their nest
  By the hawk frighted.

"Bright in her father's hall
Shields gleamed upon the wall,
Loud sang the minstrels all,
  Chanting his glory;
When of old Hildebrand
I asked his daughter's hand,
Mute did the minstrels stand
  To hear my story.

"While the brown ale he quaffed,
Loud then the champion laughed,
And as the wind-gusts waft
  The sea-foam brightly,
So the loud laugh of scorn
Out of those lips unshorn,
From the deep drinking-horn
  Blew the foam lightly.

"She was a Prince's child,
I but a Viking wild,
And though she blushed and smiled,
  I was discarded!
Should not the dove so white
Follow the sea-mew's flight?
Why did they leave that night
  Her nest unguarded?

"Scarce had I put to sea,
Bearing the maid with me,
Fairest of all was she
  Among the Norsemen!

When on the white sea-strand,
Waving his armèd hand,
Saw we old Hildebrand,
　　With twenty horsemen.

"Then launched they to the blast,
Bent like a reed each mast,
Yet we were gaining fast,
　　When the wind failed us;
And with a sudden flaw
Came round the gusty Skaw,
So that our foe we saw
　　Laugh as he hailed us.

"And as to catch the gale
Round veered the flapping sail,
'Death!' was the helmsman's hail,
　　'Death without quarter!'
Midships with iron keel
Struck we her ribs of steel;
Down her black hulk did reel
　　Through the black water!

"As with his wings aslant,
Sails the fierce cormorant,
Seeking some rocky haunt,
　　With his prey laden,—
So toward the open main,
Beating to sea again,
Through the wild hurricane,
　　Bore I the maiden.

"Three weeks we westward bore,
And when the storm was o'er,
Cloud-like we saw the shore
  Stretching to leeward;
There for my lady's bower
Built I the lofty tower,
Which, to this very hour,
  Stands looking seaward.

"There lived we many years;
Time dried the maiden's tears;
She had forgot her fears,
  She was a mother;
Death closed her mild blue eyes;
Under that tower she lies;
Ne'er shall the sun arise
  On such another!

"Still grew my bosom then,
Still as a stagnant fen!
Hateful to me were men,
  The sunlight hateful!
In the vast forest here,
Clad in my warlike gear,
Fell I upon my spear,
  Oh, death was grateful!

"Thus, seamed with many scars,
Bursting these prison bars
Up to its native stars
  My soul ascended!

There from the flowing bowl
Deep drinks the warrior's soul,
Skoal! to the Northland! *skoal!*"
Thus the tale ended.

The Discoverer of the North Cape

Othere, the old sea-captain,
  Who dwelt in Helgoland,
To King Alfred, the Lover of Truth,
Brought a snow-white walrus-tooth,
  Which he held in his brown right hand.

His figure was tall and stately;
  Like a boy's his eye appeared;
His hair was yellow as hay,
But threads of a silvery gray
  Gleamed in his tawny beard.

Hearty and hale was Othere,
  His cheek had the color of oak;
With a kind of laugh in his speech,
Like the sea-tide on a beach,
  As unto the King he spoke.

And Alfred, King of the Saxons,
  Had a book upon his knees,
And wrote down the wondrous tale
Of him who was first to sail
  Into the Arctic seas.

"So far I live to the northward,
　No man lives north of me:
To the east are wild mountain-chains,
And beyond them meres and plains;
　To the westward all is sea.

"So far I live to the northward,
　From the harbor of Skeringes-hale,
If you only sailed by day,
With a fair wind all the way,
　More than a month would you sail.

"I own six hundred reindeer,
　With sheep and swine beside;
I have tribute from the Finns,
Whalebone and reindeer-skins,
　And ropes of walrus-hide.

"I plowed the land with horses,
　But my heart was ill at ease,
For the old seafaring men
Came to me now and then,
　With their sagas of the seas;—

"Of Iceland and of Greenland,
　And the stormy Hebrides,
And the undiscovered deep;—
Oh, I could not eat nor sleep
　For thinking of those seas.

"To the northward stretched the desert,
　How far I fain would know;

So at last I sallied forth,
And three days sailed due north,
  As far as the whale-ships go.

"To the west of me was the ocean,
  To the right the desolate shore,
But I did not slacken sail
For the walrus or the whale,
  Till after three days more.

"The days grew longer and longer,
  Till they became as one,
And northward through the haze
I saw the sullen blaze
  Of the red midnight sun.

"And then uprose before me,
  Upon the water's edge,
The huge and haggard shape
Of that unknown North Cape,
  Whose form is like a wedge.

"The sea was rough and stormy,
  The tempest howled and wailed,
And the sea-fog, like a ghost,
Haunted that dreary coast,
  But onward still I sailed.

"Four days I steered to eastward,
  Four days without a night:
Round in a fiery ring
Went the great sun, O King,
  With red and lurid light."

Here Alfred, King of the Saxons,
  Ceased writing for a while;
And raised his eyes from his book,
With a strange and puzzled look,
  And an incredulous smile.

But Othere, the old sea-captain,
  He neither paused nor stirred,
Till the King listened, and then
Once more took up his pen,
  And wrote down every word.

"And now the land," said Othere,
  "Bent southward suddenly,
And I followed the curving shore
And ever southward bore
  Into a nameless sea.

"And there we hunted the walrus,
  The narwhale, and the seal;
Ha! 'twas a noble game!
And like the lightning's flame
  Flew our harpoons of steel.

"There were six of us all together,
  Norsemen of Helgoland;
In two days and no more
We killed of them threescore,
  And dragged them to the strand!"

Here Alfred the Truth-Teller
  Suddenly closed his book,

And lifted his blue eyes
With doubt and strange surmise
  Depicted in their look.

And Othere the old sea-captain
  Stared at him wild and weird,
Then smiled, till his shining teeth
Gleamed white from underneath
  His tawny, quivering beard.

And to the King of the Saxons,
  In witness of the truth,
Raising his noble head,
He stretched his brown hand, and said,
  "Behold this walrus-tooth!"

Sandalphon

Have you read in the Talmud of old,
In the Legends the Rabbins have told
  Of the limitless realms of the air,
Have you read it,—the marvelous story
Of Sandalphon, the Angel of Glory,
  Sandalphon, the Angel of Prayer?

How, erect, at the outermost gates
Of the City Celestial he waits,
  With his feet on the ladder of light,
That, crowded with angels unnumbered,
By Jacob was seen as he slumbered
  Alone in the desert at night?

The Angels of Wind and of Fire
Chant only one hymn, and expire
   With the song's irresistible stress;
Expire in their rapture and wonder,
As harp-strings are broken asunder
   By music they throb to express.

But serene in the rapturous throng,
Unmoved by the rush of the song,
   With eyes unimpassioned and slow,
Among the dead angels, the deathless
Sandalphon stands listening breathless
   To sounds that ascend from below;—

From the spirits on earth that adore,
From the souls that entreat and implore
   In the fervor and passion of prayer;
From the hearts that are broken with losses,
And weary with dragging the crosses
   Too heavy for mortals to bear.

And he gathers the prayers as he stands,
And they change into flowers in his hands,
   Into garlands of purple and red;
And beneath the great arch of the portal,
Through the streets of the City Immortal
   Is wafted the fragrance they shed.

It is but a legend, I know,—
A fable, a phantom, a show,
   Of the ancient Rabbinical lore;

Yet the old medieval tradition,
The beautiful, strange superstition,
　　But haunts me and holds me the more.

When I look from my window at night,
And the welkin above is all white,
　　All throbbing and panting with stars,
Among them majestic is standing
Sandalphon the angel, expanding
　　His pinions in nebulous bars.

And the legend, I feel, is a part
Of the hunger and thirst of the heart,
　　The frenzy and fire of the brain,
That grasps at the fruitage forbidden,
The golden pomegranates of Eden,
　　To quiet its fever and pain.

The Children's Hour

Between the dark and the daylight,
　　When the night is beginning to lower,
Comes a pause in the day's occupations,
　　That is known as the Children's Hour.

I hear in the chamber above me
　　The patter of little feet,
The sound of a door that is opened,
　　And voices soft and sweet.

173

From my study I see in the lamplight,
  Descending the broad hall stair,
Grave Alice, and laughing Allegra,
  And Edith with golden hair.

A whisper, and then a silence:
  Yet I know by their merry eyes
They are plotting and planning together
  To take me by surprise.

A sudden rush from the stairway,
  A sudden raid from the hall!
By three doors left unguarded
  They enter my castle wall!

They climb up into my turret
  O'er the arms and back of my chair;
If I try to escape, they surround me;
  They seem to be everywhere.

They almost devour me with kisses,
  Their arms about me entwine,
Till I think of the Bishop of Bingen
  In his Mouse-Tower on the Rhine!

Do you think, O blue-eyed banditti,
  Because you have scaled the wall,
Such an old mustache as I am
  Is not a match for you all!

I have you fast in my fortress,
  And will not let you depart,

But put you down into the dungeon
In the round-tower of my heart.

And there will I keep you forever,
    Yes, forever and a day,
Till the walls shall crumble to ruin,
    And molder in dust away.

Hiawatha's Childhood

From *The Song of Hiawatha*

Downward through the evening twilight,
In the days that are forgotten,
In the unremembered ages,
From the full moon fell Nokomis,
Fell the beautiful Nokomis,
She a wife, but not a mother.
    She was sporting with her women
Swinging in a swing of grapevines,
When her rival, the rejected,
Full of jealousy and hatred,
Cut the leafy swing asunder,
Cut in twain the twisted grapevines,
And Nokomis fell affrighted
Downward through the evening twilight,
On the Muskoday, the meadow,
On the prairie full of blossoms.
"See! a star falls!" said the people;
"From the sky a star is falling!"
There among the ferns and mosses,

There among the prairie lilies,
On the Muskoday the meadow,
In the moonlight and the starlight,
Fair Nokomis bore a daughter.
And she called her name Wenonah,
As the first-born of her daughters.
And the daughter of Nokomis
Grew up like the prairie lilies,
Grew a tall and slender maiden,
With the beauty of the moonlight,
With the beauty of the starlight.

   And Nokomis warned her often,
Saying oft, and oft repeating,
"O, beware of Mudjekeewis,
Of the West-Wind, Mudjekeewis;
Listen not to what he tells you;
Lie not down upon the meadow,
Stoop not down among the lilies,
Lest the West-Wind come and harm you!"

   But she heeded not the warning,
Heeded not those words of wisdom,
And the West-Wind came at evening,
Walking lightly o'er the prairie,
Whispering to the leaves and blossoms,
Bending low the flowers and grasses,
Found the beautiful Wenonah,
Lying there among the lilies,
Wooed her with his words of sweetness,
Wooed her with his soft caresses,
Till she bore a son in sorrow,
Bore a son of love and sorrow.

   Thus was born my Hiawatha,

Thus was born the child of wonder;
But the daughter of Nokomis,
Hiawatha's gentle mother,
In her anguish died deserted
By the West-Wind, false and faithless,
By the heartless Mudjekeewis.

For her daughter, long and loudly
Wailed and wept the sad Nokomis;
"O that I were dead!" she murmured,
"O that I were dead, as thou art
No more work, and no more weeping,
Wahonowin! Wahonowin!"

By the shores of Gitche Gumee.
By the shining Big-Sea-Water,
Stood the wigwam of Nokomis.
Daughter of the Moon, Nokomis,
Dark behind it rose the forest,
Rose the black and gloomy pine-trees,
Rose the firs with cones upon them;
Bright before it beat the water,
Beat the clear and sunny water,
Beat the shining Big-Sea-Water.

There the wrinkled, old Nokomis
Nursed the little Hiawatha,
Rocked him in his linden cradle,
Bedded soft in moss and rushes,
Safely bound with reindeer sinews;
Stilled his fretful wail by saying,
"Hush! the Naked Bear will get thee!"
Lulled him into slumber, singing,
"Ewa-yea! my little owlet!
Who is this, that lights the wigwam?

177

With his great eyes lights the wigwam?
Ewa-yea! my little owlet!"
    Many things Nokomis taught him
Of the stars that shine in heaven;
Showed him Ishkoodah, the comet,
Ishkoodah, with fiery tresses;
Showed the Death-Dance of the spirits,
Warriors with their plumes and war-clubs,
Flaring far away to Northward
In the frosty nights of Winter;
Showed the broad, white road in heaven,
Pathway of the ghosts, the shadows,
Running straight across the heavens,
Crowded with the ghosts, the shadows.
    At the door on Summer evenings
Sat the little Hiawatha;
Heard the whispering of the pine-trees,
Heard the lapping of the water,
Sounds of music, words of wonder:
"Minne-wawa!" said the pine-trees,
"Mudway-aushka!" said the water.
    Saw the fire-fly, Wah-wah-taysee,
Flitting through the dusk of evening,
With the twinkle of its candle
Lighting up the brakes and bushes,
And he sang the song of children,
Sang the song Nokomis taught him:
"Wah-wah-taysee, little firefly,
Little, flitting, white-fire insect,
Little, dancing, white-fire creature,
Light me with your little candle,
Ere upon my bed I lay me,

Ere in sleep I close my eyelids!"
Saw the moon rise from the water
Rippling, rounding from the water,
Saw the flecks and shadows on it,
Whispered, "What is that, Nokomis?"
And the good Nokomis answered:
"Once a warrior, very angry,
Seized his grandmother, and threw her
Up into the sky at midnight;
Right against the moon he threw her;
'Tis her body that you see there."
Saw the rainbow in the heaven,
In the eastern sky, the rainbow
Whispered, "What is that, Nokomis?"
And the good Nokomis answered:
"'Tis the heaven of flowers you see there;
All the wild-flowers of the forest,
All the lilies of the prairie,
When on earth they fade and perish,
Blossom in that heaven above us.
When he heard the owls at midnight,
Hooting, laughing in the forest,
"What is that?" he cried in terror:
"What is that?" he said, "Nokomis?"
And the good Nokomis answered:
"That is but the owl and owlet,
Talking in their native language,
Talking, scolding at each other."
Then the little Hiawatha,
Learned of every bird its language,
Learned their names and all their secrets,
How they built their nests in Summer,

Where they hid themselves in Winter,
Talked with them whene'er he met them,
Called them "Hiawatha's Chickens."
    Of all beasts he learned the language,
Learned their names and all their secrets,
How the beavers built their lodges,
Where the squirrels hid their acorns,
How the reindeer ran so swiftly,
Why the rabbit was so timid,
Talked with them whene'er he met them,
Called them "Hiawatha's Brothers."
    Then Iagoo, the great boaster,
He the marvellous story-teller,
He the traveller and the talker,
He the friend of old Nokomis,
Made a bow for Hiawatha:
From a branch of ash he made it,
From an oak-bough made the arrows,
Tipped with flint, and winged with feathers,
And the cord he made of deer-skin.
    Then he said to Hiawatha:
"Go, my son, into the forest,
Where the red deer herd together,
Kill for us a famous roebuck,
Kill for us a deer with antlers!"
    Forth into the forest straightway
All alone walked Hiawatha
Proudly, with his bow and arrows;
And the birds sang round him, o'er him,
"Do not shoot us, Hiawatha!"
Sang the Opechee, the robin,
Sang the bluebird, the Owaissa,

"Do not shoot us, Hiawatha!"
   Up the oak-tree, close beside him,
Sprang the squirrel, Adjidaumo,
In and out among the branches,
Coughed and chattered from the oak-tree,
Laughed, and said between his laughing,
"Do not shoot me, Hiawatha!"
   And the rabbit from his pathway
Leaped aside, and at a distance
Sat erect upon his haunches,
Half in fear and half in frolic,
Saying to the little hunter,
"Do not shoot me, Hiawatha!"
   But he heeded not, nor heard them,
For his thoughts were with the red deer;
On their tracks his eyes were fastened,
Leading downward to the river,
To the ford across the river,
And as one in slumber walked he.
Hidden in the alder bushes,
There he waited till the deer came,
Till he saw two antlers lifted,
Saw two eyes look from the thicket,
Saw two nostrils point to windward,
And a deer came down the pathway,
Flecked with leafy light and shadow.
And his heart within him fluttered,
Trembled like the leaves above him,
Like the birch-leaf palpitated,
As the deer came down the pathway.
   Then upon one knee uprising,
Hiawatha aimed an arrow;

Scarce a twig moved with his motion,
Scarce a leaf was stirred or rustled,
But the wary roebuck started,
Stamped with all his hoofs together,
Listened with one foot uplifted,
Leaped as if to meet the arrow;
Ah! the singing, fatal arrow,
Like a wasp it buzzed and stung him!
   Dead he lay there in the forest,
By the ford across the river;
Beat his timid heart no longer,
But the heart of Hiawatha
Throbbed and shouted and exulted,
As he bore the red deer homeward
And Iagoo and Nokomis
Hailed his coming with applauses.
From the red deer's hide Nokomis
Made a cloak for Hiawatha,
From the red deer's flesh Nokomis
Made a banquet in his honor.
All the village came and feasted,
All the guests praised Hiawatha,
Called him Strong-Heart, Soan-getaha!
Called him Loon-Heart, Mahn-go-taysee!

The Day Is Done

The day is done, and the darkness
  Falls from the wings of Night,
As a feather is wafted downward
  From an eagle in his flight.

I see the lights of the village
　　Gleam through the rain and the mist,
And a feeling of sadness comes o'er me,
　　That my soul cannot resist:

A feeling of sadness and longing,
　　That is not akin to pain,
And resembles sorrow only
　　As the mist resembles the rain.

Come, read to me some poem,
　　Some simple and heartfelt lay,
That shall soothe this restless feeling,
　　And banish the thoughts of day.

Not from the grand old masters,
　　Not from the bards sublime,
Whose distant footsteps echo
　　Through the corridors of Time.

For, like strains of martial music,
　　Their mighty thoughts suggest
Life's endless toil and endeavor;
　　And tonight I long for rest.

Read from some humbler poet,
　　Whose songs gushed from his heart,
As showers from the clouds of summer,
　　Or tears from the eyelids start;

Who, through long days of labor,
　　And nights devoid of ease,

Still heard in his soul the music
    Of wonderful melodies.

Such songs have power to quiet
    The restless pulse of care,
And come like the benediction
    That follows after prayer.

Then read from the treasured volume
    The poem of thy choice,
And lend to the rhyme of the poet
    The beauty of thy voice.

And the night shall be filled with music,
    And the cares that infest the day,
Shall fold their tents, like the Arabs,
    And as silently steal away.

JOHN GREENLEAF WHITTIER

(*1807-1892*)

Laus Deo!

*On Hearing the Bells Ring on the Passage of the
Constitutional Amendment Abolishing Slavery*

It is done!
Clang of bell and roar of gun
Send the tidings up and down.
How the belfries rock and reel!
How the great guns, peal on peal,
Fling the joy from town to town!

Ring, O bells!
Every stroke exulting tells
Of the burial hour of crime.
Loud and long, that all may hear,
Ring for every listening ear
Of Eternity and Time!

Let us kneel:
God's own voice is in that peal,
And this spot is holy ground.
Lord, forgive us! What are we,
That our eyes this glory see,
That our ears have heard the sound!

For the Lord
On the whirlwind is abroad;
In the earthquake he has spoken;
He has smitten with his thunder
The iron walls asunder,
And the gates of brass are broken!

Loud and long
Lift the old exulting song;
Sing with Miriam by the sea:
He has cast the mighty down;
Horse and rider sink and drown;
He has triumphed gloriously!

Did we dare,
In our agony of prayer,
Ask for more than He has done?
When was ever his right hand
Over any time or land
Stretched as now beneath the sun?

How they pale,
Ancient myth and song and tale,
In this wonder of our days,
When the cruel rod of war
Blossoms white with righteous law,
And the wrath of man is praise!

Blotted out!
All within and all about
Shall a fresher life begin;
Freer breathe the universe

As it rolls its heavy curse
On the dead and buried sin.

It is done!
In the circuit of the sun
Shall the sound thereof go forth.
It shall bid the sad rejoice,
It shall give the dumb a voice,
It shall belt with joy the earth!

Ring and swing,
Bells of joy! On morning's wing
Send the song of praise abroad!
With a sound of broken chains,
Tell the nations that He reigns,
Who alone is Lord and God!

My Triumph

The autumn-time has come;
On woods that dream of bloom,
And over purpling vines,
The low sun fainter shines.

The aster-flower is failing,
The hazel's gold is paling;
Yet overhead more near
The eternal stars appear!

And present gratitude
Insures the future's good,

And for the things I see
I trust the things to be;

That in the paths untrod,
And the long days of God,
My feet shall still be led,
My heart be comforted.

O living friends who love me!
O dear ones gone above me!
Careless of other fame,
I leave to you my name.

Hide it from idle praises,
Save it from evil phrases:
Why, when dear lips that spake it
Are dumb, should strangers wake it?

Let the thick curtain fall;
I better know than all
How little I have gained,
How vast the unattained.

Not by the page word-painted
Let life be banned or sainted:
Deeper than written scroll
The colors of the soul.

Sweeter than any sung
My songs that found no tongue;
Nobler than any fact
My wish that failed of act.

Others shall sing the song,
Others shall right the wrong,—
Finish what I begin,
And all I fail of win.

What matter, I or they?
Mine or another's day,
So the right word be said
And life the sweeter made?

Hail to the coming singers!
Hail to the brave light-bringers!
Forward I reach and share
All that they sing and dare.

The airs of heaven blow o'er me;
A glory shines before me
Of what mankind shall be,—
Pure, generous, brave and free.

A dream of man and woman
Diviner but still human,
Solving the riddle old,
Shaping the Age of Gold!

The love of God and neighbor;
An equal-handed labor;
The richer life, where beauty
Walks hand in hand with duty.

Ring, bells in unreared steeples,
The joy of unborn peoples!

Sound, trumpets far off blown,
Your triumph is my own!

Parcel and part of all,
I keep the festival,
Fore-reach the good to be,
And share the victory.

I feel the earth move sunward,
I join the great march onward,
And take, by faith, while living,
My freehold of thanksgiving.

The Eternal Goodness

O friends! with whom my feet have trod
   The quiet aisles of prayer,
Glad witness to your zeal for God
   And love of man I bear.

I trace your lines of argument;
   Your logic linked and strong
I weigh as one who dreads dissent,
   And fears a doubt as wrong.

But still my human hands are weak
   To hold your iron creeds:
Against the words ye bid me speak
   My heart within me pleads.

Who fathoms the Eternal Thought?
　Who talks of scheme and plan?
The Lord is God! He needeth not
　The poor device of man.

I walk with bare, hushed feet the ground
　Ye tread with boldness shod;
I dare not fix with mete and bound
　The love and power of God.

Ye praise His justice; even such
　His pitying love I deem:
Ye seek a king; I fain would touch
　The robe that hath no seam.

Ye see the curse which overbroods
　A world of pain and loss;
I hear our Lord's beatitudes
　And prayer upon the cross.

More than your schoolmen teach, within
　Myself, alas! I know:
Too dark ye cannot paint the sin,
　Too small the merit show.

I bow my forehead to the dust,
　I veil mine eyes for shame,
And urge, in trembling self-distrust,
　A prayer without a claim.

I see the wrong that round me lies,
　I feel the guilt within;

I hear, with groan and travail-cries,
   The world confess its sin.

Yet, in the maddening maze of things,
   And tossed by storm and flood,
To one fixed trust my spirit clings;
   I know that God is good!

Not mine to look where cherubim
   And seraphs may not see,
But nothing can be good in him
   Which evil is in me.

The wrong that pains my soul below
   I dare not throne above,
I know not of his hate,—I know
   His goodness and his love.

I dimly guess from blessings known
   Of greater out of sight,
And, with the chastened Psalmist, own
   His judgments too are right.

I long for household voices gone,
   For vanished smiles I long,
But God hath led my dear ones on,
   And he can do no wrong.

I know not what the future hath
   Of marvel or surprise,
Assured alone that life and death
   His mercy underlies.

And if my heart and flesh are weak
　To bear an untried pain,
The bruised reed he will not break,
　But strengthen and sustain.

No offering of my own I have,
　Nor works my faith to prove;
I can but give the gifts he gave,
　And plead his love for love.

And so beside the Silent Sea
　I wait the muffled oar;
No harm from him can come to me
　On ocean or on shore.

I know not where his islands lift
　Their fronded palms in air;
I only know I cannot drift
　Beyond his love and care.

O brothers! if my faith is vain,
　If hopes like these betray,
Pray for me that my feet may gain
　The sure and safer way.

And Thou, O Lord! by whom are seen
　Thy creatures as they be,
Forgive me if too close I lean
　My human heart on thee!

Ichabod[1]

So fallen! so lost! the light withdrawn
    Which once he wore!
The glory from his gray hairs gone
    Forevermore!

Revile him not—the Tempter hath
    A snare for all;
And pitying tears, not scorn and wrath,
    Befit his fall!

Oh, dumb be passion's stormy rage,
    When he who might
Have lighted up and led his age,
    Falls back in night.

Scorn! would the angels laugh, to mark
    A bright soul driven,
Fiend-goaded, down the endless dark,
    From hope and heaven!

Let not the land once proud of him
    Insult him now,
Nor brand with deeper shame his dim,
    Dishonored brow.

[1] Ichabod: From the Hebrew (*I Samuel IV: 21*), literally: "the glory is departed." Whittier thus characterized Webster because of his "compromise" speech of March 7, 1850.

But let its humbled sons, instead,
    From sea to lake,
A long lament, as for the dead,
    In sadness make.

Of all we loved and honored, naught
    Save power remains—
A fallen angel's pride of thought,
    Still strong in chains.

All else is gone; from those great eyes
    The soul has fled:
When faith is lost, when honor dies,
    The man is dead!

Then, pay the reverence of old days
    To his dead fame;
Walk backward, with averted gaze,
    And hide the shame!

Barbara Frietchie

Up from the meadows rich with corn,
Clear in the cool September morn,

The clustered spires of Frederick stand
Green-walled by the hills of Maryland.

Round about them orchards sweep,
Apple and peach tree fruited deep,

Fair as the garden of the Lord
To the eyes of the famished rebel horde,

On that pleasant morn of the early fall
When Lee marched over the mountain wall;

Over the mountains winding down,
Horse and foot, into Frederick town.

Forty flags with their silver stars,
Forty flags with their crimson bars,

Flapped in the morning wind: the sun
Of noon looked down, and saw not one.

Up rose old Barbara Frietchie then,
Bowed with her fourscore years and ten;

Bravest of all in Frederick town,
She took up the flag the men hauled down;

In her attic window the staff she set,
To show that one heart was loyal yet.

Up the street came the rebel tread,
Stonewall Jackson riding ahead.

Under his slouched hat left and right
He glanced; the old flag met his sight.

"Halt!"—the dust-brown ranks stood fast,
"Fire"—out blazed the rifle-blast.

It shivered the window, pane and sash;
It rent the banner with seam and gash.

Quick as it fell, from the broken staff
Dame Barbara snatched the silken scarf.

She leaned far out on the window-sill,
And shook it forth with a royal will.

"Shoot, if you must, this old gray head,
But spare your country's flag," she said.

A shade of sadness, a blush of shame,
Over the face of the leader came;

The nobler nature within him stirred
To life at that woman's deed and word;

"Who touches a hair of yon gray head
Dies like a dog! March on!" he said.

All day long through Frederick street
Sounded the tread of marching feet:

All day long that free flag tossed
Over the heads of the rebel host.

Ever its torn folds rose and fell
On the loyal winds that loved it well;

And through the hill-gaps sunset light
Shone over it with a warm good-night.

197

Barbara Frietchie's work is o'er,
And the Rebel rides on his raids no more.

Honor to her! and let a tear
Fall, for her sake, on Stonewall's bier.

Over Barbara Frietchie's grave,
Flag of Freedom and Union, wave!

Peace and order and beauty draw
Round thy symbol of light and law;

And ever the stars above look down
On thy stars below in Frederick town!

The Waiting

I wait and watch: before my eyes
　　Methinks the night grows thin and gray;
I wait and watch the eastern skies
To see the golden spears uprise
　　Beneath the oriflamme of day!

Like one whose limbs are bound in trance
　　I hear the day-sounds swell and grow,
And see across the twilight glance,
Troop after troop, in swift advance,
　　The shining ones with plumes of snow!

I know the errand of their feet,
　　I know what mighty work is theirs;

I can but lift up hands unmeet
The threshing-floors of God to beat,
    And speed them with unworthy prayers.

I will not dream in vain despair
    The steps of progress wait for me:
The puny leverage of a hair
The planet's impulse well may spare,
    A drop of dew the tided sea.

The loss, if loss there be, is mine,
    And yet not mine if understood;
For one shall grasp and one resign,
One drink life's rue, and one its wine,
    And God shall make the balance good.

O power to do! O baffled will!
    O prayer and action! ye are one.
Who may not strive, may yet fulfil
The harder task of standing still,
    And good but wished with God is done!

The Trailing Arbutus

I wandered lonely where the pine-trees made
Against the bitter East their barricade,
    And, guided by its sweet
Perfume, I found, within a narrow dell,
The trailing spring flower tinted like a shell
    Amid dry leaves and mosses at my feet.

199

From under dead boughs, for whose loss the pines
Moaned ceaseless overhead, the blossoming vines
  Lifted their glad surprise,
While yet the bluebird smoothed in leafless trees
His feathers ruffled by the chill sea-breeze,
  And snow-drifts lingered under April skies.

As, pausing, o'er the lonely flower I bent,
I thought of lives thus lowly, clogged and pent,
  Which yet find room
Through care and cumber, coldness and decay,
To lend a sweetness to the ungenial day,
  And make the sad earth happier for their bloom.

Maud Muller

Maud Muller, on a summer's day,
Raked the meadow sweet with hay.

Beneath her torn hat glowed the wealth
Of simple beauty and rustic health.

Singing, she wrought, and her merry glee
The mock-bird echoed from his tree.

But, when she glanced to the far-off town,
White from its hill-slope looking down,

The sweet song died, and a vague unrest
And a nameless longing filled her breast—

A wish that she hardly dared to own,
For something better than she had known.

The Judge rode slowly down the lane,
Smoothing his horse's chestnut mane.

He drew his bridle in the shade
Of the apple trees, to greet the maid.

And ask a draught from the spring that flowed
Through the meadow across the road.

She stooped where the cool spring bubbled up,
And filled for him her small tin cup,

And blushed as she gave it, looking down
On her feet so bare, and her tattered gown.

"Thanks!" said the Judge, "a sweeter draught
From a fairer hand was never quaffed."

He spoke of the grass and flowers and trees,
Of the singing birds and the humming bees;

Then talked of the haying, and wondered whether
The cloud in the west would bring foul weather.

And Maud forgot her brier-torn gown,
And her graceful ankles bare and brown;

And listened, while a pleased surprise
Looked from her long-lashed hazel eyes.

At last, like one who for delay
Seeks a vain excuse, he rode away.

Maud Muller looked and sighed: "Ah, me!
That I the Judge's bride might be!

"He would dress me up in silks so fine,
And praise and toast me at his wine.

"My father should wear a broadcloth coat;
My brother should sail a painted boat.

"I'd dress my mother so grand and gay,
And the baby should have a new toy each day.

"And I'd feed the hungry and clothe the poor,
And all should bless me who left our door."

The Judge looked back as he climbed the hill,
And saw Maud Muller standing still.

"A form more fair, a face more sweet,
Ne'er hath it been my lot to meet.

"And her modest answer and graceful air
Show her wise and good as she is fair.

"Would she were mine, and I today,
Like her, a harvester of hay:

"No doubtful balance of rights and wrongs,
Nor weary lawyers with endless tongues,

"But low of cattle and song of birds,
And health and quiet and loving words."

But he thought of his sisters proud and cold,
And his mother vain of her rank and gold.

So, closing his heart, the Judge rode on,
And Maud was left in the field alone.

But the lawyers smiled that afternoon,
When he hummed in court an old love-tune;

And the young girl mused beside the well,
Till the rain on the unraked clover fell.

He wedded a wife of richest dower,
Who lived for fashion, as he for power.

Yet oft, in his marble hearth's bright glow,
He watched a picture come and go:

And sweet Maud Muller's hazel eyes
Looked out in their innocent surprise.

Oft, when the wine in his glass was red,
He longed for the wayside well instead;

And closed his eyes on his garnished rooms,
To dream of meadows and clover-blooms.

And the proud man sighed, with a secret pain:
"Ah, that I were free again!

"Free as when I rode that day,
Where the barefoot maiden raked her hay."

She wedded a man unlearned and poor,
And many children played round her door.

But care and sorrow, and childbirth pain,
Left their traces on heart and brain.

And oft, when the summer sun shone hot
On the new-mown hay in the meadow lot,

And she heard the little spring brook fall
Over the roadside, through the wall,

In the shade of the apple tree again
She saw a rider draw his rein.

And, gazing down with timid grace,
She felt his pleased eyes read her face.

Sometimes her narrow kitchen walls
Stretched away into stately halls;

The weary wheel to a spinnet turned,
The tallow candle an astral burned,

And for him who sat by the chimney lug,
Dozing and grumbling o'er pipe and mug,

A manly form at her side she saw,
And joy was duty and love was law.

Then she took up her burden of life again,
Saying only, "It might have been."

Alas for maiden, alas for Judge,
For rich repiner and household drudge!

God pity them both! and pity us all,
Who vainly the dreams of youth recall.

For all sad words of tongue or pen,
The saddest are these: "It might have been!"

Ah, well! for us all some sweet hope lies
Deeply buried from human eyes;

And, in the hereafter, angels may
Roll the stone from its grave away!

The Barefoot Boy

Blessings on thee, little man,
Barefoot boy, with cheek of tan!
With thy turned-up pantaloons,
And thy merry whistled tunes;
With thy red lip, redder still
Kissed by strawberries on the hill;
With the sunshine on thy face,
Through thy torn brim's jaunty grace:
From my heart I give thee joy—
I was once a barefoot boy!
Prince thou art—the grown-up man

Only is republican.
Let the million-dollared ride!
Barefoot, trudging at his side,
Thou has more than he can buy,
In the reach of ear and eye—
Outward sunshine, inward joy:
Blessings on thee, barefoot boy!

O, for boyhood's painless play,
Sleep that wakes in laughing day,
Health that mocks the doctor's rules,
Knowledge never learned of schools,
Of the wild bee's morning chase,
Of the wild-flower's time and place,
Flight of fowl and habitude
Of the tenants of the wood;
How the tortoise bears his shell,
How the woodchuck digs his cell,
And the ground-mole sinks his well;
How the robin feeds her young,
How the oriole's nest is hung;
Where the whitest lilies blow,
Where the freshest berries grow,
Where the ground-nut trails its vine,
Where the wood-grape's clusters shine;
Of the black wasp's cunning way,
Mason of his walls of clay,
And the architectural plans
Of gray hornet artisans!—
For, eschewing books and tasks,
Nature answers all he asks;
Hand in hand with her he walks,

Face to face with her he talks,
Part and parcel of her joy,—
Blessings on the barefoot boy!

O, for boyhood's time of June,
Crowding years in one brief moon,
When all things I heard or saw,
Me, their master, waited for.
I was rich in flowers and trees,
Humming-birds and honey-bees;
For my sport the squirrel played,
Plied the snouted mole his spade;
For my taste the blackberry cone
Purpled over hedge and stone;
Laughed the brook for my delight
Through the day and through the night,
Whispering at the garden wall,
Talked with me from fall to fall;
Mine the sand-rimmed pickerel pond,
Mine the walnut slopes beyond,
Mine, on bending orchard trees,
Apples of Hesperides!
Still, as my horizon grew,
Larger grew my riches too;
All the world I saw or knew
Seemed a complex Chinese toy,
Fashioned for a barefoot boy!

O, for festal dainties spread,
Like my bowl of milk and bread,—
Pewter spoon and bowl of wood,
On the door-stone, gray and rude!

O'er me, like a regal tent,
Cloudy-ribbed, the sunset bent,
Purple-curtained, fringed with gold,
Looped in many a wind-swung fold;
While for music came the play
Of the pied frogs' orchestra;
And, to light the noisy choir,
Lit the fly his lamp of fire.
I was monarch: pomp and joy
Waited on the barefoot boy!

Cheerily, then, my little man,
Live and laugh, as boyhood can!
Though the flinty slopes be hard,
Stubble-speared the new-morn sward,
Every morn shall lead thee through
Fresh baptisms of the dew;
Every evening from thy feet
Shall the cool wind kiss the heat:
All too soon these feet must hide
In the prison cells of pride,
Lose the freedom of the sod,
Like a colt's for work be shod,
Made to tread the mills of toil,
Up and down in ceaseless moil:
Happy if their track be found
Never on forbidden ground;
Happy if they sink not in
Quick and treacherous sands of sin.
Ah! that thou couldst know thy joy,
Ere it passes, barefoot boy!

Skipper Ireson's Ride

Of all the rides since the birth of time,
Told in story or sung in rime—
On Apuleius's Golden Ass,
Or one-eyed Calendar's horse of brass,
Witch astride of a human hack,
Islam's prophet on Al-Borák—
The strangest ride that ever was sped
Was Ireson's out from Marblehead!
   Old Floyd Ireson, for his hard heart,
    Tarred and feathered and carried in a cart
     By the women o' Morble'ead!"

Body of Turkey, head of owl,
Wings a-droop like a rained-on fowl,
Feathered and ruffled in every part,
Skipper Ireson stood in the cart.
Scores of women, old and young,
Strong of muscle, and glib of tongue,
Pushed and pulled up the rocky lane,
Shouting and singing the shrill refrain:
   "Here's Flud Oirson, fur his horrd horrt,
    Torr'd an' futherr'd an' corr'd in a corrt
     By the women of Marblehead!

Wrinkled scolds with hands on hips,
Girls in bloom of cheek and lips,
Wild-eyed, free-limbed, such as chase
Bacchus round some antique vase,

209

Brief of skirt, with ankles bare,
Loose of kerchief and loose of hair,
With conch-shells blowing and fish-horns' twang,
Over and over the Maenads sang:
    "Here's Flud Oirson, fur his horrd horrt,
    Torr'd an' futherr'd an' corr'd in a corrt
    By the women o' Morble'ead!"

Small pity for him!—He sailed away
From a leaking ship in Chaleur Bay—
Sailed away from a sinking wreck,
With his own town's-people on her deck!
"Lay by! lay by!" they called to him.
Back he answered, "Sink or swim!
Brag of your catch of fish again!"
And off he sailed through the fog and rain!
    Old Floyd Ireson, for his hard heart.
    Tarred and feathered and carried in a cart
    By the women of Marblehead!

Fathoms deep in dark Chaleur
That wreck shall lie forevermore.
Mother and sister, wife and maid,
Looked from the rocks of Marblehead
Over the moaning and rainy sea—
Looked for the coming that might not be!
What did the winds and the sea-birds say
Of the cruel captain who sailed away?—
    Old Floyd Ireson, for his hard heart,
    Tarred and feathered and carried in a cart
    By the women of Marblehead.

Through the street, on either side,
Up flew windows, doors swung wide;
Sharp-tongued spinsters, old wives gray,
Treble lent the fish-horn's bray.
Sea-worn grandsires, cripple-bound,
Hulks of old sailors run aground,
Shook head, and fist, and hat, and cane,
And cracked with curses the hoarse refrain:
   "Here's Flud Oirson, fur his horrd horrt,
   Torr'd an' futherr'd an' corr'd in a corrt
     By the women o' Morble'ead!"

Sweetly along the Salem road
Bloom of orchard and lilac showed.
Little the wicked skipper knew
Of the fields so green and the sky so blue.
Riding there in his sorry trim,
Like an Indian idol glum and grim,
Scarcely he seemed the sound to hear
Of voices shouting far and near:
   "Here's Flud Oirson, fur his horrd horrt,
   Torr'd an' futherr'd an' corr'd in a corrt
     By the women o' Morble'ead!"

"Hear me, neighbors!" at last he cried—
"What to me is this noisy ride?
What is the shame that clothes the skin
To the nameless horror that lives within?
Waking or sleeping, I see a wreck,
And hear a cry from a reeling deck!
Hate me and curse me,—I only dread
The hand of God and the face of the dead!"

Said old Floyd Ireson, for his hard heart,
Tarred and feathered and carried in a cart
   By the women of Marblehead!

Then the wife of the skipper lost at sea
Said, "God has touched him! why should we?"
Said an old wife mourning her only son,
"Cut the rogue's tether and let him run!"
So with soft relentings and rude excuse,
Half scorn, half pity, they cut him loose,
And gave him a cloak to hide him in,
And left him alone with his shame and sin.
   Poor Floyd Ireson, for his hard heart,
   Tarred and feathered and carried in a cart
   By the women of Marblehead!

From "Snow-Bound"

(A Winter Idyl)

The sun that brief December day
Rose cheerless over hills of gray,
And, darkly circled, gave at noon
A sadder light than waning moon.
Slow tracing down the thickening sky
Its mute and ominous prophecy,
A portent seeming less than threat,
It sank from sight before it set.
A chill no coat, however stout,
Of homespun stuff could quite shut out,

A hard, dull bitterness of cold,
   That checked, mid-vein, the circling race
   Of life-blood in the sharpened face,
The coming of the snow-storm told.
The wind blew east: we heard the roar
Of Ocean on his wintry shore,
And felt the strong pulse throbbing there
Beat with low rhythm our inland air.

Meanwhile we did our nightly chores,—
Brought in the wood from out of doors,
Littered the stalls, and from the mows
Raked down the herd's-grass for the cows;
Heard the horse whinnying for his corn;
And, sharply clashing horn on horn,
Impatient down the stanchion rows
The cattle shake their walnut bows;
While, peering from his early perch
Upon the scaffold's pole of birch,
The cock his crested helmet bent
And down his querulous challenge sent.

Unwarmed by any sunset light
The gray day darkened into night,
A night made hoary with the swarm
And whirl-dance of the blinding storm,
As zigzag wavering to and fro,
Crossed and recrossed the winged snow:
And ere the early bedtime came
The white drift piled the window-frame,
And through the glass the clothes-line posts
Looked in like tall and sheeted ghosts.

So all night long the storm roared on:
The morning broke without a sun;
In tiny spherule traced with lines
Of Nature's geometric signs,
In starry flake and pellicle,
All day the hoary meteor fell;
And, when the second morning shone,
We looked upon a world unknown,
On nothing we could call our own.
Around the glistening wonder bent
The blue walls of the firmament,
No cloud above, no earth below,—
A universe of sky and snow!
The old familiar sights of ours
Took marvelous shapes; strange domes and towers
Rose up where sty or corn-crib stood,
Or garden-wall or belt of wood;
A smooth white mound the brush-pile showed,
A fenceless drift what once was road;
The bridle-post an old man sat
With loose-flung coat and high cocked hat;
The well-curb had a Chinese roof;
And even the long sweep, high aloof,
In its slant splendor, seemed to tell
Of Pisa's leaning miracle.

A prompt, decisive man, no breath
Our father wasted: "Boys, a path!"
Well pleased, (for when did farmer boy
Count such a summons less than joy?)
Our buskins on our feet we drew;
With mittened hands, and caps drawn low,

To guard our necks and ears from snow,
We cut the solid whiteness through.
And, where the drift was deepest, made
A tunnel walled and overlaid
With dazzling crystal: we had read
Of rare Aladdin's wondrous cave,
And to our own his name we gave,
With many a wish the luck were ours
To test his lamp's supernal powers.
We reached the barn with merry din,
And roused the prisoned brutes within.
The old horse thrust his long head out,
And grave with wonder gazed about;
The cock his lusty greeting said,
And forth his speckled harem led;
The oxen lashed their tails, and hooked,
And mild reproach of hunger looked;
The hornèd patriarch of the sheep,
Like Egypt's Amun roused from sleep,
Shook his sage head with gesture mute,
And emphasized with stamp of foot.

All day the gusty north-wind bore
The loosening drift its breath before;
Low circling round its southern zone,
The sun through dazzling snow-mist shone.
No church-bell lent its Christian tone
To the savage air, no social smoke
Curled over woods of snow-hung oak.
A solitude made more intense
By dreary-voicèd elements,
The shrieking of the mindless wind,

The moaning tree-boughs swaying blind,
And on the glass the unmeaning beat
Of ghostly finger-tips of sleet.
Beyond the circle of our hearth
No welcome sound of toil or mirth
Unbound the spell, and testified
Of human life and thought outside.
We minded that the sharpest ear
The buried brooklet could not hear,
The music of whose liquid lip
Had been to us companionship,
And, in our lonely life, had grown
To have an almost human tone.

As night drew on, and, from the crest
Of wooded knolls that ridged the west,
The sun, a snow-blown traveller, sank
From sight beneath the smothering bank,
We piled, with care, our nightly stack
Of wood against the chimney-back,—
The oaken log, green, huge, and thick,
And on its top the stout back-stick;
The knotty forestick laid apart,
And filled between with curious art
The ragged brush; then, hovering near,
We watched the first red blaze appear,
Heard the sharp crackle, caught the gleam
On whitewashed wall and sagging beam,
Until the old, rude-furnished room
Burst, flower-like, into rosy bloom;
While radiant with a mimic flame
Outside the sparkling drift became,

And through the bare-boughed lilac-tree
Our own warm hearth seemed blazing free.
The crane and pendent trammels showed;
The Turks' heads on the andirons glowed;
While childish fancy, prompt to tell
The meaning of the miracle,
Whispered the old rhyme: *"Under the tree,*
When fire outdoors burns merrily,
There the witches are making tea."

The moon above the eastern wood
Shone at its full; the hill-range stood
Transfigured in the silver flood,
Its blown snows flashing cold and keen,
Dead white, save where some sharp ravine
Took shadow, or the somber green
Of hemlocks turned to pitchy black
Against the whiteness at their back.
For such a world and such a night
Most fitting that unwarming light,
Which only seemed where'er it fell
To make the coldness visible.

Shut in from all the world without,
We sat the clean-winged hearth about,
Content to let the north-wind roar
In baffled rage at pane and door,
While the red logs before us beat
The frost-line back with tropic heat;
And ever, when a louder blast
Shook beam and rafter as it passed,
The merrier up its roaring draught

The great throat of the chimney laughed;
The house-dog on his paws outspread
Laid to the fire his drowsy head,
The cat's dark silhouette on the wall
A couchant tiger's seemed to fall;
And, for the winter fireside meet,
Between the andirons' straddling feet,
The mug of cider simmered slow,
The apples sputtered in a row,
And, close at hand, the basket stood
With nuts from brown October's wood.

What matter how the night behaved?
What matter how the north-wind raved?
Blow high, blow low, not all its snow
Could quench out hearth-fire's ruddy glow.
O Time and Change!—with hair as gray
As was my sire's that winter day,
How strange it seems, with so much gone
Of life and love, to still live on!
Ah, brother! only I and thou
Are left of all that circle now,—
The dear home faces whereupon
That fitful firelight paled and shone.
Henceforward, listen as we will,
The voices of that hearth are still;
Look where we may, the wide earth o'er,
Those lighted faces smile no more.
We tread the paths their feet have worn,
    We sit beneath their orchard-trees,
    We hear, like them, the hum of bees
And rustle of the bladed corn;

We turn the pages that they read,
    Their written words we linger o'er,
But in the sun they cast no shade,
No voice is heard, no sign is made,
    No step is on the conscious floor!
Yet Love will dream, and Faith will trust,
(Since He who knows our need is just,)
That somehow, somewhere, meet we must.
Alas for him who never sees
The stars shine through his cypress-trees!
Who, hopeless, lays his dead away,
Nor looks to see the breaking day
Across the mournful marbles play!
Who hath not learned, in hours of faith,
    The truth to flesh and sense unknown,
That Life is ever lord of Death,
    And Love can never lose its own!

. . . . . .

Next morn we wakened with the shout
Of merry voices high and clear;
And saw the teamsters drawing near
To break the drifted highways out.
Down the long hillside treading slow
We saw the half-buried oxen go,
Shaking the snow from heads uptost,
Their straining nostrils white with frost.
Before our door the straggling train
Drew up, an added team to gain.
The elders threshed their hands a-cold,
    Passed, with the cider-mug, their jokes
    From lip to lip; the younger folks
Down the loose snow-banks, wrestling, rolled,

Then toiled again the cavalcade
  O'er windy hill, through clogged ravine,
  And woodland paths that wound between
Low drooping pine-boughs winter-weighed.
From every barn a team afoot,
At every house a new recruit,
Where, drawn by Nature's subtlest law,
Haply the watchful young men saw
Sweet doorway pictures of the curls
And curious eyes of merry girls,
Lifting their hands in mock defense
Against the snow-ball's compliments,
And reading in each missive tossed
The charm with Eden never lost.

The Moral Warfare

When Freedom, on her natal day,
Within her war-rocked cradle lay,
An iron race around her stood,
Baptized her infant brow in blood
And, through the storm which round her swept,
Their constant ward and watching kept.

Then, where our quiet herds repose,
The roar of baleful battle rose,
And brethren of a common tongue
To mortal strife as tigers sprung,
And every gift on Freedom's shrine
Was man for beast, and blood for wine!

Our fathers to their graves have gone;
Their strife is past—their triumph won;
But sterner trials wait the race
Which rises in their honored place—
A moral warfare with the crime
And folly of an evil time.

So let it be. In God's own might
We gird us for the coming fight,
And, strong in Him whose cause is ours
In conflict with unholy powers,
We grasp the weapons He has given,—
The Light, and Truth, and Love of Heaven!

THOMAS HOLLEY CHIVERS

(*1809-1858*)

Apollo

What are stars but hieroglyphics of God's glory writ in light-
   ning
   On the wide-unfolded pages of the azure scroll above?
But the quenchless apotheoses of thoughts forever brightening
   In the mighty Mind immortal of the God whose name is
      Love?
Diamond letters sculptured, rising, on the azure ether pages,
   That now sing to one another, unto one another shine—
God's eternal Scripture talking, through the midnight, to the
      Ages,
   Of the life that is immortal, of the life that is divine—
   Life that *cannot* be immortal, but the life that is divine.

Like some deep, impetuous river from the fountains everlasting,
   Down the serpentine soft valley of the vistas of all Time,
Over cataracts of adamant uplifted into mountains,
   Soared his soul to God in thunder on the wings of thought
      sublime.
With the rising golden glory of the sun in ministrations,
   Making oceans metropolitan of splendor for the dawn—
Piling pyramid on pyramid of music for the nations—
   Sings the Angel who sits shining everlasting in the sun,
   For the stars which are the echoes of the shining of the sun.

Like the lightnings piled on lightnings, ever rising, never reach-
      ing,

In one monument of glory toward the golden gates of God—
Voicing out themselves in thunder upon thunder in their preach-
      ing,
Piled this Cyclops up his Epic where the Angels never trod.
Like the fountains everlasting that for evermore are flowing
    From the throne within the center of the City built on high,
With their genial irrigation life for evermore bestowing—
    Flows his lucid, liquid river through the gardens of the sky,
    For the stars forever blooming in the gardens of the sky.

Song To Isa Singing

Upon thy lips now lies
    The music-dew of love;
And in thy deep blue eyes,
    More mild than Heaven above—
    The meekness of the dove.

More sweet than the perfume
    Of snow-white jessamine
When it is first in bloom,
    Is that sweet breath of thine,
    Which mingles now with mine.

Like an Æolian sound
    Out of an ocean shell,
Which fills the air around
    With music such as fell
    From lips of Israfel;

223

Over thy lips now flow
  Out of thy heart, for me,
A song which none can know
  But him who hopes to be
  Forever more with thee.

And like the snow-white dove
  Frightened from earth at even—
On tempests borne above—
  My swift-winged soul is driven
  Upon thy song to heaven!

EDGAR ALLAN POE

(*1809-1849*)

To Helen

Helen, thy beauty is to me
   Like those Nicéan barks of yore,
That gently, o'er a perfumed sea,
   The weary, way-worn wanderer bore
   To his own native shore.

On desperate seas long wont to roam,
   Thy hyacinth hair, thy classic face,
Thy Naiad airs have brought me home
   To the glory that was Greece,
   And the grandeur that was Rome.

Lo! in yon brilliant window-niche
   How statue-like I see thee stand,
The agate lamp within thy hand!
   Ah, Psyche, from the regions which
   Are Holy-Land!

A Dream Within a Dream

Take this kiss upon thy brow!
And, in parting from you now,
Thus much let me avow—
You are not wrong, to deem

That my days have been a dream;
Yet if Hope has flown away
In a night, or in a day,
In a vision, or in none,
Is it therefore the less *gone*?
All that we see or seem
Is but a dream within a dream.

I stand amid the roar
Of a surf-tormented shore,
And I hold within my hand
Grains of the golden sand—
How few! yet how they creep
Through my fingers to the deep,
While I weep—while I weep!

O God! can I not grasp
Them with a tighter clasp?
O God! can I not save
One from the pitiless wave?
Is *all* that we see or seem
But a dream within a dream?

Israfel

*And the angel Israfel, whose heart-strings are a lute, and who has the sweetest voice of all God's creatures.—*KORAN.

In Heaven a spirit doth dwell
   "Whose heart-strings are a lute";
None sing so wildly well

As the angel Israfel,
And the giddy stars (so legends tell)
Ceasing their hymns, attend the spell
   Of his voice, all mute.

Tottering above
   In her highest noon,
   The enamored Moon
Blushes with love,
   While, to listen, the red levin
   (With the rapid Pleiads, even,
   Which were seven,)
   Pauses in Heaven.

And they say (the starry choir
   And the other listening things)
That Israfeli's fire
Is owing to that lyre
   By which he sits and sings—
The trembling living wire
   Of those unusual strings.

But the skies that angel trod,
   Where deep thoughts are a duty,
Where Love's a grown-up God,
   Where the Houri glances are
Imbued with all the beauty
   Which we worship in a star.

Therefore, thou art not wrong,
   Israfeli, who despisest
An unimpassioned song;

To thee the laurels belong,
  Best bard, because the wisest!
Merrily live, and long!

The ecstasies above
  With thy burning measures suit—
Thy grief, thy joy, thy hate, thy love,
  With the fervor of thy lute—
  Well may the stars be mute!

Yes, Heaven is thine; but this
  Is a world of sweets and sours;
  Our flowers are merely—flowers,
And the shadow of thy perfect bliss
  Is the sunshine of ours.

If I could dwell
Where Israfel
  Hath dwelt, and he where I,
He might not sing so wildly well
  A mortal melody,
While a bolder note than this might swell
  From my lyre within the sky.

The Haunted Palace

(From "The Fall of the House of Usher")

In the greenest of our valleys
  By good angels tenanted,
Once a fair and stately palace—

Radiant palace—reared its head.
In the monarch Thought's dominion—
    It stood there!
Never seraph spread a pinion
    Over fabric half so fair!

Banners yellow, glorious, golden,
    On its roof did float and flow,
(This—all this—was in the olden
    Time long ago),
And every gentle air that dallied,
    In that sweet day,
Along the ramparts plumed and pallid,
    A winged odor went away.

Wanderers in that happy valley,
    Through two luminous windows, saw
Spirits moving musically,
    To a lute's well-tuned law,
Round about a throne where, sitting,
    (Porphyrogene!)
In state his glory well befitting,
    The ruler of the realm was seen.

And all with pearl and ruby glowing
    Was the fair palace door,
Through which came flowing, flowing, flowing,
    And sparkling evermore,
A troop of Echoes, whose sweet duty
    Was but to sing,
In voices of surpassing beauty,
    The wit and wisdom of their king.

But evil things, in robes of sorrow,
   Assailed the monarch's high estate.
(Ah, let us mourn!—for never morrow
   Shall dawn upon him, desolate!)
And round about his home the glory
   That blushed and bloomed,
Is but a dim-remembered story
   Of the old time entombed.

And travellers, now, within that valley,
   Through the red-litten windows see
Vast forms, that move fantastically
   To a discordant melody,
While, like a ghastly rapid river,
   Through the pale door
A hideous throng rush out forever
   And laugh—but smile no more.

The City in the Sea

Lo! Death has reared himself a throne
In a strange city lying alone
Far down within the dim West,
Where the good and the bad and the worst and the best
Have gone to their eternal rest.
There shrines and palaces and towers
(Time-eaten towers that tremble not!)
Resemble nothing that is ours.
Around, by lifting winds forgot,
Resignedly beneath the sky
The melancholy waters lie.

No rays from the holy heaven come down
On the long night-time of that town;
But light from out the lurid sea
Streams up the turrets silently—
Gleams up the pinnacles far and free—
Up domes—up spires—up kingly halls—
Up fanes—up Babylon-like walls—
Up shadowy long-forgotten bowers
Of sculptured ivy and stone flowers—
Up many and many a marvelous shrine
Whose wreathed friezes intertwine
The viol, the violet, and the vine.

Resignedly beneath the sky
The melancholy waters lie.
So blend the turrets and shadows there
That all seem pendulous in air,
While from a proud tower in the town
Death looks gigantically down.

There open fanes and gaping graves
Yawn level with the luminous waves;
But not the riches there that lie
In each idol's diamond eye—
Not the gaily-jeweled dead
Tempt the waters from their bed;
For no ripples curl, alas!
Along that wilderness of glass—
No swellings tell that winds may be
Upon some far-off happier sea—
No heavings hint that winds have been
On seas less hideously serene.

But lo, a stir is in the air!
The wave—there is a movement there!
As if the towers had thrust aside,
In slightly sinking, the dull tide—
As if their tops had feebly given
A void within the filmy Heaven.

The waves have now a redder glow—
The hours are breathing faint and low—
And when, amid no earthly moans,
Down, down that town shall settle hence,
Hell, rising from a thousand thrones,
Shall do it reverence.

Annabel Lee

It was many and many a year ago,
    In a kingdom by the sea,
That a maiden there lived whom you may know
    By the name of Annabel Lee;—
And this maiden she lived with no other thought
    Than to love and be loved by me.

She was a child and I was a child,
    In this kingdom by the sea,
But we loved with a love that was more than love—
    I and my Annabel Lee—
With a love that the winged seraphs of Heaven
    Coveted her and me.

232

And this was the reason that, long ago,
   In this kingdom by the sea,
O wind blew out of a cloud, by night
   Chilling my Annabel Lee;
So that her highborn kinsmen came
   And bore her away from me,
To shut her up in a sepulchre
   In this kingdom by the sea.

The angels, not half so happy in Heaven,
   Went envying her and me:
Yes! that was the reason (as all men know,
   In this kingdom by the sea)
That the wind came out of the cloud, chilling
   And killing my Annabel Lee.

But our love it was stronger by far than the love
   Of those who were older than we—
   Of many far wiser than we—
And neither the angels in Heaven above
   Nor the demons down under the sea,
Can ever dissever my soul from the soul
   Of the beautiful Annabel Lee:—

For the moon never beams without bringing me dreams
   Of the beautiful Annabel Lee;
And the stars never rise but I see the bright eyes
   Of the beautiful Annabel Lee;
And so, all the night-tide, I lie down by the side
Of my darling, my darling, my life and my bride,
   In her sepulchre there by the sea—
   In her tomb by the sounding sea.

233

To One in Paradise

Thou wast all that to me, love,
  For which my soul did pine—
A green isle in the sea, love,
  A fountain and a shrine,
All wreathed with fairy fruits and flowers,
  And all the flowers were mine.

Ah, dream too bright to last!
  Ah, starry Hope! that didst arise
But to be overcast!
  A voice from out the Future cries,
"On! on!"—but o'er the Past
  (Dim gulf!) my spirit hovering lies
Mute, motionless, aghast!

For, alas! alas! with me
  The light of Life is o'er!
No more—no more—no more—
  (Such language holds the solemn sea
To the sands upon the shore)
  Shall bloom the thunder-blasted tree,
Or the stricken eagle soar!

And all my days are trances,
  And all my nightly dreams
Are where thy gray eye glances,
  And where thy footstep gleams—
In what ethereal dances,
  By what eternal streams.

Romance

Romance, who loves to nod and sing,
With drowsy head and folded wing,
Among the green leaves as they shake
Far down within some shadowy lake,
To me a painted paroquet
Hath been—a most familiar bird—
Taught me my alphabet to say—
To lisp my very earliest word
While in the wild wood I did lie,
A child—with a most knowing eye.

Of late, eternal condor years
So shake the very Heaven on high
With tumult as they thunder by,
I have no time for idle cares
Through gazing on the unquiet sky.
And when an hour with calmer wings
Its down upon my spirit flings—
That little time with lyre and rhyme
To while away—forbidden things!
My heart would feel to be a crime
Unless it trembled with the strings.

To Science

Science! true daughter of Old Time thou art!
Who alterest all things with thy peering eyes.
Why preyest thou thus upon the poet's heart,

Vulture, whose wings are dull realities?
How should he love thee? or how deem thee wise,
Who wouldst not leave him in his wandering
To seek for treasure in the jewelled skies,
Albeit he soared with an undaunted wing?
Hast thou not dragged Diana from her car?
And driven the Hamadryad from the wood
To seek a shelter in some happier star?
Hast thou not torn the Naiad from her flood,
The Elfin from the green grass, and from me
The summer dream beneath the tamarind tree?

The Raven

Once upon a midnight dreary, while I pondered, weak and
    weary,
Over many a quaint and curious volume of forgotten lore,—
While I nodded, nearly napping, suddenly there came a tapping,
As of some one gently rapping, rapping at my chamber door.
" 'Tis some visitor," I muttered, "tapping at my chamber door;
        Only this, and nothing more."

Ah, distinctly I remember, it was in the bleak December,
And each separate dying ember wrought its ghost upon the floor.
Eagerly I wished the morrow; vainly I had sought to borrow
From my books surcease of sorrow,—sorrow for the lost
    Lenore,—
For the rare and radiant maiden whom the angels named
    Lenore,—
        Nameless here forevermore.

And the silken, sad, uncertain rustling of each purple curtain
Thrilled me,—filled me with fantastic terrors never felt before;
So that now, to still the beating of my heart, I stood repeating,
" 'Tis some visitor entreating entrance at my chamber door,—
Some late visitor entreating entrance at my chamber door;
   That it is, and nothing more."

Presently my soul grew stronger; hesitating then no longer,
"Sir," said I, "or madam, truly your forgiveness I implore;
But the fact is, I was napping, and so gently you came rapping,
And so faintly you came tapping, tapping at my chamber door,
That I scarce was sure I heard you."—Here I opened wide the
  door;
   Darkness there, and nothing more.

Deep into that darkness peering, long I stood there, wondering,
  fearing,
Doubting, dreaming dreams no mortal ever dared to dream
  before;
But the silence was unbroken, and the darkness gave no token,
And the only word there spoken was the whispered word
  "Lenore!"
This I whispered, and an echo murmured back the word
  "Lenore!"
   Merely this, and nothing more.

Back into the chamber turning, all my soul within me burning,
Soon again I heard a tapping, something louder than before:
"Surely," said I, "surely that is something at my window-lattice;
Let me see then what thereat is, and this mystery explore,—
Let my heart be still a moment, and this mystery explore;—
   'Tis the wind, and nothing more."

Open then I flung the shutter, when, with many a flirt and
    flutter,
In there stepped a stately raven of the saintly days of yore.
Not the least obeisance made he; not an instant stopped or stayed
    he;
But, with mien of lord or lady, perched above my chamber
    door,—
Perched upon a bust of Pallas, just above my chamber door,—
        Perched, and sat, and nothing more.

Then this ebony bird beguiling my sad fancy into smiling,
By the grave and stern decorum of the countenance it wore,
"Though thy crest be shorn and shaven, thou," I said, "art sure
    no craven;
Ghastly, grim, and ancient raven, wandering from the nightly
    shore,
Tell me what thy lordly name is on the night's Plutonian
    shore?"
        Quoth the raven, "Nevermore!"

Much I marvelled this ungainly fowl to hear discourse so
    plainly,
Though its answer little meaning, little relevancy bore;
For we cannot help agreeing that no living human being
Ever yet was blessed with seeing bird above his chamber door,
Bird or beast upon the sculptured bust above his chamber door,
        With such name as "Nevermore!"

But the raven, sitting lonely on the placid bust, spoke only
That one word, as if his soul in that one word he did outpour.
Nothing further then he uttered,—not a feather then he flut-
    tered,—

Till I scarcely more than muttered, "Other friends have flown
    before,—
On the morrow he will leave me, as my hopes have flown
    before."
        Then the bird said, "Nevermore!"

Startled at the stillness, broken by reply so aptly spoken,
"Doubtless," said I, "what it utters is its only stock and store,
Caught from some unhappy master, whom unmerciful disaster
Followed fast and followed faster, till his song one burden bore,
Till the dirges of his hope that melancholy burden bore,—
        Of 'Nevermore,—nevermore!'"

But the raven still beguiling all my sad soul into smiling,
Straight I wheeled a cushioned seat in front of bird and bust and
    door,
Then, upon the velvet sinking, I betook myself to linking
Fancy unto fancy, thinking what this ominous bird of yore—
What this grim, ungainly, ghastly, gaunt, and ominous bird of
    yore—
        Meant in croaking "Nevermore!"

This I sat engaged in guessing, but no syllable expressing
To the fowl whose fiery eyes now burned into my bosom's core;
This and more I sat divining, with my head at ease reclining
On the cushion's velvet lining that the lamplight gloated o'er,
But whose velvet violet lining, with the lamplight gloating o'er,
        She shall press—ah! nevermore!

Then methought the air grew denser, perfumed from an unseen
    censer,
Swung by seraphim, whose footfalls tinkled on the tufted floor.

"Wretch," I cried, "thy God hath lent thee,—by these angels he
    hath sent thee
Respite,—respite and nepenthe from the memories of Lenore!
Quaff, O, quaff this kind nepenthe, and forget this lost Lenore!"
        Quoth the raven, "Nevermore!"

"Prophet!" said I, "thing of evil!—prophet still, if bird or devil!
Whether tempter sent, or whether tempest tossed thee here
    ashore,
Desolate yet all undaunted, on this desert land enchanted,—
On this home by horror haunted,—tell me truly, I implore,—
Is there—is there balm in Gilead?—tell me,—tell me, I
    implore!"
        Quoth the raven, "Nevermore!"

"Prophet!" said I, "thing of evil!—prophet still, if bird or devil!
By that heaven that bends above us,—by that God we both
    adore,
Tell this soul with sorrow laden, if, within the distant Aidenn,
It shall clasp a sainted maiden, whom the angels name Lenore,
Clasp a fair and radiant maiden, whom the angels name
    Lenore!"
        Quoth the raven, "Nevermore!"

"Be that word our sign of parting, bird or fiend!" I shrieked,
    upstarting,—
"Get thee back into the tempest and the night's Plutonian shore!
Leave no black plume as a token of that lie thy soul hath spoken!
Leave my loneliness unbroken!—quit the bust above my door!
Take thy beak from out my heart, and take thy form from off
    my door!"
        Quoth the raven, "Nevermore!"

And the raven, never flitting, still is sitting, still is sitting
On the pallid bust of Pallas, just above my chamber door;
And his eyes have all the seeming of a demon that is dreaming,
And the lamplight o'er him streaming throws his shadow on the
    floor;
And my soul from out that shadow that lies floating on the floor
    Shall be lifted—*nevermore!*

Ulalume

The skies they were ashen and sober;
    The leaves they were crisped and sere—
    The leaves they were withering and sere;
It was night in the lonesome October
    Of my most immemorial year;
It was hard by the dim lake of Auber,
    In the misty mid region of Weir—
It was down by the dank tarn of Auber,
    In the ghoul-haunted woodland of Weir.

Here once, through an alley Titanic,
    Of cypress, I roamed with my Soul—
    Of cypress, with Psyche, my Soul.
These were days when my heart was volcanic
    As the scoriac rivers that roll—
    As the lavas that restlessly roll
Their sulphurous currents down Yaanek
    In the ultimate climes of the pole—
That groan as they roll down Mount Yaanek
    In the realms of the boreal pole.

241

Our talk had been serious and sober,
>But our thoughts they were palsied and sere—
>Our memories were treacherous and sere—
For we knew not the month was October,
>And we marked not the night of the year—
>(Ah, night of all nights in the year!)
We noted not the dim lake of Auber—
>(Though once we had journeyed down here),
Remembered not the dank tarn of Auber,
>Nor the ghoul-haunted woodland of Weir.

And now, as the night was senescent,
>And star-dials pointed to morn—
>As the star-dials hinted of morn—
At the end of our path a liquescent
>And nebulous lustre was born,
Out of which a miraculous crescent
>Arose with a duplicate horn—
Astarte's bediamonded crescent
>Distinct with its duplicate horn.

And I said—"She is warmer than Dian:
>She rolls through an ether of sighs—
>She revels in a region of sighs:
She has seen that the tears are not dry on
>These cheeks, where the worm never dies,
And has come past the stars of the Lion,
>To point us the path to the skies—
>To the Lethean peace of the skies—
Come up, in despite of the Lion,
>To shine on us with her bright eyes—

Come up through the lair of the Lion,
    With love in her luminous eyes."

But Psyche, uplifting her finger,
    Said—"Sadly this star I mistrust—
    Her pallor I strangely mistrust:—
Oh, hasten!—oh, let us not linger!
    Oh, fly!—let us fly!—for we must."
In terror she spoke, letting sink her
    Wings until they trailed in the dust—
In agony sobbed, letting sink her
    Plumes till they trailed in the dust—
    Till they sorrowfully trailed in the dust.

I replied—"This is nothing but dreaming:
    Let us on by this tremulous light!
    Let us bathe in this crystalline light!
Its Sybilic splendour is beaming
    With Hope and in Beauty to-night:—
    See!—it flickers up the sky through the night!
Ah, we safely may trust to its gleaming,
    And be sure it will lead us aright—
We safely may trust to a gleaming
    That cannot but guide us aright,
    Since it flickers up to Heaven through the night."

Thus I pacified Psyche and kissed her,
    And tempted her out of her gloom—
    And conquered her scruples and gloom;
And we passed to the end of the vista,
    But were stopped by the door of a tomb—
    By the door of a legended tomb;

243

And I said—"What is written, sweet sister,
  On the door of this legended tomb?"
  She replied—"Ulalume—Ulalume—
  'Tis the vault of thy lost Ulalume!"

Then my heart it grew ashen and sober
  As the leaves that were crisped and sere—
  As the leaves that were withering and sere—
And I cried—"It was surely October
  On *this* very night of last year
  That I journeyed—I journeyed down here—
  That I brought a dread burden down here—
  On this night of all nights in the year,
  Ah, what demon has tempted me here?
Well I know, now, this dim lake of Auber—
  This misty mid region of Weir—
Well I know, now, this dank tarn of Auber,
  This ghoul-haunted woodland of Weir."

To F——

Beloved! amid the earnest woes
  That crowd around my earthly path—
(Drear path, alas! where grows
Not even one lonely rose)—
  My soul at least a solace hath
In dreams of thee, and therein knows
An Eden of bland repose.

And thus thy memory is to me
  Like some enchanted far-off isle

In some tumultuous sea—
Some ocean throbbing far and free
   With storms—but where meanwhile
Serenest skies continually
   Just o'er that one bright island smile.

To My Mother

Because I feel that, in the Heavens above,
   The angels, whispering to one another,
Can find, among their burning terms of love,
   None so devotional as that of "Mother,"
Therefore by that dear name I long have called you—
   You who are more than mother unto me,
And fill my heart of hearts, where Death installed you,
   In setting my Virginia's spirit free.
My mother—my own mother, who died early,
   Was but the mother of myself; but you
Are mother to the one I loved so dearly,
   And thus are dearer than the mother I knew
By that infinity with which my wife
   Was dearer to my soul than its soul-life.

For Annie

Thank Heaven! the crisis—
   The danger is past,
And the lingering illness
   Is over at last—
And the fever called "Living"
   Is conquered at last

245

Sadly, I know
   I am shorn of my strength,
And no muscle I move
   As I lie at full length—
But no matter!—I feel
   I am better at length.

And I rest so composedly,
   Now, in my bed,
That any beholder
   Might fancy me dead—
Might start at beholding me,
   Thinking me dead.

The moaning and groaning,
   The sighing and sobbing,
Are quieted now,
   With that horrible throbbing
At heart:—ah, that horrible,
   Horrible throbbing!

The sickness—the nausea—
   The pitiless pain—
Have ceased, with the fever
   That maddened my brain—
With the fever called "Living"
   That burned in my brain.

And oh! of all tortures
   That torture the worst
Has abated—the terrible
   Torture of thirst

For the naphthaline river
   Of Passion accurst:—
I have drunk of a water
   That quenches all thirst:—

Of a water that flows,
   With a lullaby sound,
From a spring but a very few
   Feet under ground—
From a cavern not very far
   Down under ground.

And ah! let it never
   Be foolishly said
That my room it is gloomy
   And narrow my bed;
For man never slept
   In a different bed—
And, to *sleep*, you must slumber
   In just such a bed.

My tantalized spirit
   Here blandly reposes.
Forgetting, or never
   Regretting its roses—
Its old agitations
   Of myrtles and roses;
For now, while so quietly
   Lying, it fancies
A holier odor
   About it, of pansies—

247

A rosemary odor,
  Commingled with pansies—
With rue and the beautiful
  Puritan pansies.

And so it lies happily,
  Bathing in many
A dream of the truth
  And the beauty of Annie—
Drowned in a bath
  Of the tresses of Annie.

She tenderly kissed me,
  She fondly caressed,
And then I fell gently
  To sleep on her breast—
Deeply to sleep
  From the heaven of her breast.

When the light was extinguished
  She covered me warm,
And she prayed to the angels
  To keep me from harm—
To the queen of the angels
  To shield me from harm.

And I lie so composedly,
  Now, in my bed,
(Knowing her love)
  That you fancy me dead—
And I rest so contentedly,
  Now, in my bed,

(With her love at my breast)
  That you fancy me dead—
That you shudder to look at me,
  Thinking me dead.—

But my heart it is brighter
  Than all of the many
Stars in the sky,
  For it sparkles with Annie—
It glows with the light
  Of the love of my Annie—
With the thought of the light
  Of the eyes of my Annie.

Dream-Land

By a route obscure and lonely,
Haunted by ill angels only,
Where an Eidolon, named NIGHT,
On a black throne reigns upright,
I have reached these lands but newly
From an ultimate dim Thule—
From a wild weird clime that lieth, sublime,
  Out of SPACE—out of TIME.

Bottomless vales and boundless floods,
And chasms, and caves, and Titan woods,
With forms that no man can discover
For the tears that drip all over;
Mountains toppling evermore
Into seas without a shore;

249

Seas that restlessly aspire,
Surging, unto skies of fire;
Lakes that endlessly outspread
Their lone waters—lone and dead,—
Their still waters—still and chilly
With the snows of the lolling lily.

By the lakes that thus outspread
Their lone waters, lone and dead,—
Their sad waters, sad and chilly
With the snows of the lolling lily,—
By the mountains—near the river
Murmuring lowly, murmuring ever,—
By the grey woods,—by the swamp
Where the toad and the newt encamp,—
By the dismal tarns and pools
 Where dwell the Ghouls,—
By each spot the most unholy—
In each nook most melancholy,—
There the traveller meets, aghast,
Sheeted Memories of the Past—
Shrouded forms that start and sigh
As they pass the wanderer by—
White-robed forms of friends long given,
In agony, to the Earth—and Heaven.

For the heart whose woes are legion
'Tis a peaceful, soothing region—
For the spirit that walks in shadow
'Tis—oh 'tis an Eldorado!
But the traveller, travelling through it,
May not—dare not openly view it;

Never its mysteries are exposed
To the weak human eye unclosed;
So wills its King, who hath forbid
The uplifting of the fringèd lid;
And thus the sad Soul that here passes
Beholds it but through darkened glasses.

By a route obscure and lonely,
Haunted by ill angels only,
Where an Eidolon, named NIGHT,
On a black throne reigns upright,
I have wandered home but newly
From this ultimate dim Thule.

The Sleeper

At midnight, in the month of June,
I stand beneath the mystic moon.
An opiate vapour, dewy, dim,
Exhales from out her golden rim,
And, softly dripping, drop by drop,
Upon the quiet mountain top,
Steals drowsily and musically
Into the universal valley.
The rosemary nods upon the grave;
The lily lolls upon the wave;
Wrapping the fog about its breast,
The ruin moulders into rest;
Looking like Lethe, see! the lake
A conscious slumber seems to take,
And would not, for the world, awake.

251

All Beauty sleeps!—and lo! where lies
(Her casement open to the skies)
Irene, with her Destinies!
Oh, lady bright! can it be right—
This window open to the night?
The wanton airs, from the tree-top,
Laughingly through the lattice drop—
The bodiless airs, a wizard rout,
Flit through thy chamber in and out,
And wave the curtain canopy
So fitfully—so fearfully—
Above the closed and fringed lid
'Neath which thy slumb'ring soul lies hid,
That, o'er the floor and down the wall,
Like ghosts the shadows rise and fall!
Oh, lady dear, hast thou no fear?
Why and what art thou dreaming here?
Sure thou art come o'er far-off seas,
A wonder to these garden trees!
Strange is thy pallor, strange thy dress!
Strange, above all, thy length of tress,
And this all-solemn silentness!

The lady sleeps! Oh, may her sleep,
Which is enduring, so be deep!
Heaven have her in its sacred keep!
This chamber changed for one more holy,
This bed for one more melancholy,
I pray to God that she may lie
Forever with unopened eye,
While the dim sheeted ghosts go by!

My love, she sleeps! Oh, may her sleep,
As it is lasting, so be deep!
Soft may the worms about her creep!
Far in the forest, dim and old,
For her may some tall vault unfold—
Some vault that oft hath flung its black
And winged panels fluttering back,
Triumphant, o'er the crested palls,
Of her grand family funerals—
Some sepulchre, remote, alone,
Against whose portal she hath thrown
In childhood many an idle stone—
Some tomb from out whose sounding door
She ne'er shall force an echo more,
Thrilling to think, poor child of sin!
It was the dead who groaned within.

Sonnet: Silence

There are some qualities—some incorporate things,
  That have a double life, which thus is made
A type of that twin entity which springs
  From matter and light, evinced in solid and shade.
There is a twofold Silence—sea and shore—
  Body and soul. One dwells in lonely places,
  Newly with grass o'ergrown; some solemn graces,
Some human memories and tearful lore,
Render him terrorless: his name's "No More."
He is the corporate Silence: dread him not!
  No power hath he of evil in himself;

But should some urgent fate (untimely lot!)
   Bring thee to meet his shadow (nameless elf,
That haunteth the lone regions where hath trod
No foot of man), commend thyself to God!

The Lake. To ——

In spring of youth it was my lot
To haunt of the wide world a spot
The which I could not love the less—
So lovely was the loneliness
Of a wild lake, with black rock bound,
And the tall pines that towered around.

But when the Night had thrown her pall
Upon that spot, as upon all,
And the mystic wind went by
Murmuring in melody—
Then—ah, then, I would awake
To the terror of the lone lake.

Yet that terror was not fright,
But a tremulous delight—
A feeling not the jewelled mine
Could teach or bribe me to define
Nor Love—although the Love were thine.

Death was in that poisonous wave,
And in its gulf a fitting grave
For him who thence could solace bring

To his lone imagining—
Whose solitary soul could make
An Eden of that dim lake.

The Valley of Unrest

Once it smiled a silent dell
Where the people did not dwell;
They had gone unto the wars,
Trusting to the mild-eyed stars,
Nightly, from their azure towers,
To keep watch above the flowers,
In the midst of which all day
The red sun-light lazily lay.
Now each visitor shall confess
The sad valley's restlessness.
Nothing there is motionless—
Nothing save the airs that brood
Over the magic solitude.
Ah, by no wind are stirred those trees
That palpitate like the chill seas
Around the misty Hebrides!
Ah, by no wind those clouds are driven
That rustle through the unquiet Heaven
Uneasily, from morn til even,
Over the violets there that lie
In myriad types of the human eye
Over the lilies there that wave
And weep above a nameless grave!
They wave:—from out their fragrant tops

Eternal dews come down in drops.
They weep:—from off their delicate stems
Perennial tears descend in gems.

Eldorado

Gaily bedight,
A gallant knight,
In sunshine and in shadow,
Had journeyed long,
Singing a song,
In search of Eldorado.

But he grew old—
This knight so bold—
And o'er his heart a shadow
Fell as he found
No spot of ground
That looked like Eldorado.

And, as his strength
Failed him at length,
He met a pilgrim shadow—
"Shadow," said he,
"Where can it be—
This land of Eldorado?"

"Over the Mountains
Of the Moon,
Down the Valley of the Shadow,

Ride, boldly ride,"
The shade replied—
"If you seek for Eldorado!"

Alone

From childhood's hour I have not been
As others were—I have not seen
As others saw—I could not bring
My passions from a common spring—
From the same source I have not taken
My sorrow—I could not awaken
My heart to joy at the same tone—
And all I loved—I loved alone—
Then—in my childhood—in the dawn
Of a most stormy life—was drawn
From every depth of good and ill
The mystery which binds me still—
From the torrent, or the fountain—
From the red cliff of the mountain—
From the sun that round me roll'd
In its autumn tint of gold—
From the lightning in the sky
As it passed me flying by—
From the thunder and the storm—
And the cloud that took the form
(When the rest of Heaven was blue)
Of a demon in my view.

OLIVER WENDELL HOLMES

(*1809-1894*)

The Chambered Nautilus

This is the ship of pearl, which, poets feign,
  Sails the unshadowed main,—
  The venturous bark that flings
On the sweet summer wind its purpled wings
In gulfs enchanted, where the Siren sings,
  And coral reefs lie bare,
Where the cold sea-maids rise to sun their streaming hair.

Its webs of living gauze no more unfurl;
  Wrecked is the ship of pearl!
  And every chambered cell,
Where its dim dreaming life was wont to dwell,
As the frail tenant shaped his growing shell,
  Before thee lies revealed,—
Its irised ceiling rent, its sunless crypt unsealed!

Year after year beheld the silent toil
  That spread his lustrous coil;
  Still, as the spiral grew,
He left the past year's dwelling for the new,
Stole with soft step its shining archway through,
  Built up its idle door,
Stretched in his last-found home, and knew the old no more.

258

Thanks for the heavenly message brought by thee,
   Child of the wandering sea,
   Cast from her lap, forlorn!
From thy dead lips a clearer note is born
Than ever Triton blew from wreathed horn!
   While on mine ear it rings,
Through the deep caves of thought I hear a voice that sings,—

Build thee more stately mansions, O my soul,
   As the swift seasons roll!
   Leave thy low-vaulted past!
Let each new temple, nobler than the last,
Shut thee from heaven with a dome more vast,
   Till thou at length art free,
Leaving thine outgrown shell by life's unresting sea!

Old Ironsides

Ay, tear her tattered ensign down!
   Long has it waved on high,
And many an eye has danced to see
   That banner in the sky;
Beneath it rung the battle shout,
   And burst the cannon's roar;—
The meteor of the ocean air
   Shall sweep the clouds no more!

Her deck, once red with heroes' blood,
   Where knelt the vanquished foe,
When winds were hurrying o'er the flood,
   And waves were white below,

259

No more shall feel the victor's tread,
    Or know the conquered knee;—
The harpies of the shore shall pluck
    The eagle of the sea!

O better that her shattered hulk
    Should sink beneath the wave;
Her thunders shook the mighty deep,
    And there should be her grave;
Nail to the mast her holy flag,
    Set every threadbare sail,
And give her to the god of storms,
    The lightning and the gale!

Dorothy Q.

A Family Portrait

Grandmother's mother: her age, I guess,
Thirteen summers, or something less;
Girlish bust, but womanly air;
Smooth, square forehead with uprolled hair;
Lips that lover has never kissed;
Taper fingers and slender wrist;
Hanging sleeves of stiff brocade;
So they painted the little maid.

On her hand a parrot green
Sits unmoving and broods serene.
Hold up the canvas full in view,—
Look! there's a rent the light shines through,

Dark with a century's fringe of dust,—
That was a Red-Coat's rapier-thrust!
Such is the tale the lady old,
Dorothy's daughter's daughter, told.

Who the painter was none may tell,—
One whose best was not over well;
Hard and dry, it must be confessed,
Flat as a rose that has long been pressed;
Yet in her cheek the hues are bright,
Dainty colors of red and white,
And in her slender shape are seen
Hint and promise of stately mien.

Look not on her with eyes of scorn,—
Dorothy Q. was a lady born!
Ay! since the galloping Normans came,
England's annals have known her name;
And still to the three-hilled rebel town
Dear is that ancient name's renown,
For many a civic wreath they won,
The youthful sire and the gray-haired son.

O Damsel Dorothy! Dorothy Q.!
Strange is the gift that I owe to you;
Such a gift as never a king
Save to daughter or son might bring,—
All my tenure of heart and hand,
All my title to house and land;
Mother and sister and child and wife
And joy and sorrow and death and life!

What if a hundred years ago
Those close-shut lips had answered No,
When forth the tremulous question came
That cost the maiden her Norman name,
And under the folds that look so still
The bodice swelled with the bosom's thrill?
Should I be I, or would it be
One tenth another, to nine tenths me?

Soft is the breath of a maiden's YES:
Not the light gossamer stirs with less;
But never a cable that holds so fast
Through all the battles of wave and blast,
And never an echo of speech or song
That lives in the babbling air so long!
There were tones in the voice that whispered then
You may hear to-day in a hundred men.

O lady and lover, how faint and far
Your images hover,—and here we are
Solid and stirring in flesh and bone,—
Edward's and Dorothy's—all their own,—
A goodly record for Time to show
Of a syllable spoken so long ago!—
Shall I bless you, Dorothy, or forgive
For the tender whisper that bade me live?

It shall be a blessing, my little maid!
I will heal the stab of the Red-Coat's blade,
And freshen the gold of the tarnished frame,
And gild with a rhyme your household name;
So you shall smile on us brave and bright

As first you greeted the morning's light,
And live untroubled by woes and fears
Through a second youth of a hundred years.

The Last Leaf

I saw him once before,
As he passed by the door,
   And again
The pavement stones resound,
As he totters o'er 'the ground
   With his cane.

They say that in his prime,
Ere the pruning-knife of Time
   Cut him down,
Not a better man was found
By the Crier on his round
   Through the town.

But now he walks the streets,
And he looks at all he meets
   Sad and wan,
And he shakes his feeble head,
That it seems as if he said,
   "They are gone."

The mossy marbles rest
On the lips that he has prest
   In their bloom,

263

And the names he loved to hear
Have been carved for many a year
  On the tomb.

My grandmamma has said—
Poor old lady, she is dead
  Long ago—
That he had a Roman nose,
And his cheek was like a rose
  In the snow.

But now his nose is thin,
And it rests upon his chin
  Like a staff,
And a crook is in his back,
And a melancholy crack
  In his laugh.

I know it is a sin
For me to sit and grin
  At him here;
But the old three-cornered hat,
And the breeches, and all that,
  Are so queer!

And if I should live to be
The last leaf upon the tree
  In the spring,
Let them smile, as I do now,
At the old forsaken bough
  Where I cling.

The Deacon's Masterpiece

Or, the Wonderful "One-Hoss Shay"

A Logical Story

Have you heard of the wonderful one-hoss shay,
That was built in such a logical way
It ran a hundred years to a day,
And then, of a sudden, it — ah, but stay,
I'll tell you what happened without delay,
Scaring the parson into fits,
Frightening people out of their wits,—
Have you ever heard of that, I say?

Seventeen hundred and fifty-five.
Georgius Secundus was then alive,—
Snuffy old drone from the German hive.
That was the year when Lisbon-town
Saw the earth open and gulp her down,
And Braddock's army was done so brown,
Left without a scalp to its crown.
It was on the terrible Earthquake-day
That the Deacon finished the one-hoss shay.

Now in building of chaises, I tell you what,
There is always *somewhere* a weakest spot,—
In hub, tire, felloe, in spring or thill,
In panel, or crossbar, or floor, or sill,
In screw, bolt, thoroughbrace,—lurking still,
Find it somewhere you must and will,—

Above or below, or within or without,—
And that's the reason, beyond a doubt,
That a chaise *breaks down*, but doesn't *wear out*.

But the Deacon swore (as Deacons do,
With an "I dew vum," or an "I tell *yeou*,")
He would build one shay to beat the taown
'n' the keounty 'n' all the kentry raoun';
It should be so built that it *couldn'* break daown:
—"Fur," said the Deacon, " 't's mighty plain
Thut the weakes' place mus' stan' the strain;
'n' the way t' fix it, uz I maintain,
      Is only jest
T' make that place uz strong uz the rest."

So the Deacon inquired of the village folk
Where he could find the strongest oak,
That couldn't be split nor bent nor broke,—
That was for spokes and floor and sills;
He sent for lancewood to make the thills;
The crossbars were ash, from the straightest trees,
The panels of white-wood, that cuts like cheese,
But lasts like iron for things like these;
The hubs of logs from the "Settler's ellum,"—
Last of its timber,—they couldn't sell 'em,
Never an axe had seen their chips,
And the wedges flew from between their lips,
Their blunt ends frizzled like celery-tips;
Step and prop-iron, bolt and screw,
Spring, tire, axle, and linchpin too,
Steel of the finest, bright and blue;
Thoroughbrace bison-skin, thick and wide;

Boot, top, dasher, from tough old hide
Found in the pit when the tanner died.
That was the way he "put her through."—
"There!" said the Deacon, "naow she'll dew!"

Do! I tell you, I rather guess
She was a wonder, and nothing less!
Colts grew horses, beards turned gray,
Deacon and deaconess dropped away,
Children and grandchildren—where were they?
But there stood the stout old one-hoss shay
As fresh as on Lisbon-earthquake-day!
EIGHTEEN HUNDRED;—it came and found
The Deacon's masterpiece strong and sound.
Eighteen hundred increased by ten;—
"Hahnsum kerridge" they called it then.
Eighteen hundred and twenty came;—
Running as usual; much the same.
Thirty and forty at last arrive,
And then come fifty, and FIFTY-FIVE.

Little of all we value here
Wakes on the morn of its hundredth year
Without both feeling and looking queer.
In fact, there's nothing that keeps its youth,
So far as I know, but a tree and truth.
(This is a moral that runs at large;
Take it.—You're welcome.—No extra charge.)
FIRST OF NOVEMBER,—the Earthquake-day—
There are traces of age in the one-hoss shay,
A general flavor of mild decay,
But nothing local, as one may say,

There couldn't be,—for the Deacon's art
Had made it so like in every part
That there wasn't a chance for one to start.
For the wheels were just as strong as the thills,
And the floor was just as strong as the sills,
And the panels just as strong as the floor,
And the whipple-tree neither less nor more,
And the back-crossbar as strong as the fore,
And spring and axle and hub *encore*.
And yet, *as a whole*, it is past a doubt
In another hour it will be *worn out*!

First of November, 'Fifty-five!
This morning the parson takes a drive.
Now, small boys, get out of the way!
Here comes the wonderful one-hoss shay,
Drawn by a rat-tailed, ewe-necked bay.
"Huddup!" said the parson.—Off went they.

The parson was working his Sunday's text,—
Had got to *fifthly*, and stopped perplexed
At what the—Moses—was coming next.
All at once the horse stood still,
Close by the meet'n'-house on the hill.
—First a shiver, and then a thrill,
Then something decidedly like a spill,—
And the parson was sitting upon a rock,
At half past nine by the meet'n'-house clock,—
Just the hour of the Earthquake shock!
—What do you think the parson found,
When he got up and stared around?
The poor old chaise in a heap or mound,

As if it had been to the mill and ground!
You see, of course, if you're not a dunce,
How it went to pieces all at once,—
All at once, and nothing first,—
Just as bubbles do when they burst.

End of the wonderful one-hoss shay.
Logic is logic. That's all I say.

The Ballad of the Oysterman

It was a tall young oysterman lived by the river-side,
His shop was just upon the bank, his boat was on the tide;
The daughter of a fisherman, that was so straight and slim,
Lived over on the other bank, right opposite to him.

It was the pensive oysterman that saw a lovely maid,
Upon a moonlight evening, a sitting in the shade;
He saw her wave her handkerchief, as much as if to say,
"I'm wide awake, young oysterman, and all the folks away."

Then up arose the oysterman, and to himself said he,
"I guess I'll leave the skiff at home, for fear that folks should
        see;
I read it in the story-book, that, for to kiss his dear,
Leander swam the Hellespont,—and I will swim this here."

And he has leaped into the waves, and crossed the shining stream,
And he has clambered up the bank, all in the moonlight gleam;
O there were kisses sweet as dew, and words as soft as rain,—
But they have heard her father's step, and in he leaps again!

269

Out spoke the ancient fisherman,—"O what was that, my
    daughter?"
" 'Twas nothing but a pebble, sir, I threw into the water."
"And what is that, pray tell me, love, that paddles off so fast?"
"It's nothing but a porpoise, sir, that's been a swimming past."

Out spoke the ancient fisherman,—"Now bring me my harpoon!
I'll get into my fishing-boat, and fix the fellow soon."
Down fell that pretty innocent, as falls a snow-white lamb,
Her hair drooped round her pallid cheeks, like seaweed on a
    clam.

Alas for those two loving ones! she waked not from her swound,
And he was taken with the cramp, and in the waves was
    drowned;
But Fate has metamorphosed them, in pity of their woe,
And now they keep an oyster-shop for mermaids down below.

My Aunt

My aunt! my dear unmarried aunt!
    Long years have o'er her flown;
Yet still she strains the aching clasp
    That binds her virgin zone;
I know it hurts her,—though she looks
    As cheerful as she can;
Her waist is ampler than her life,
    For life is but a span.

My aunt! my poor deluded aunt!
    Her hair is almost gray;

Why will she train that winter curl
     In such a spring-like way?
How can she lay her glasses down,
     And say she reads as well,
When, through a double convex lens,
     She just makes out to spell?

Her father—grandpapa! forgive
     This erring lip its smiles—
Vowed she should make the finest girl
     Within a hundred miles;
He sent her to a stylish school;
     'Twas in her thirteenth June;
And with her, as the rules required,
     "Two towels and a spoon."

They braced my aunt against a board,
     To make her straight and tall;
They laced her up, they starved her down,
     To make her light and small;
They pinched her feet, they singed her hair,
     They screwed it up with pins;—
O never mortal suffered more
     In penance for her sins.

So, when my precious aunt was done,
     My grandsire brought her back;
(By daylight, lest some rabid youth
     Might follow on the track;)
"Ah!" said my grandsire, as he shook
     Some powder in his pan,

"What could this lovely creature do
  Against a desperate man!"

Alas! nor chariot, nor barouche,
  Nor bandit cavalcade,
Tore from the trembling father's arms
  His all-accomplished maid.
For her how happy had it been!
  And Heaven had spared to me
To see one sad, ungathered rose
  On my ancestral tree.

The Height of the Ridiculous

I wrote some lines once on a time
  In wondrous merry mood,
And thought, as usual, men would say
  They were exceeding good.

They were so queer, so very queer,
  I laughed as I would die;
Albeit, in the general way,
  A sober man am I.

I called my servant, and he came;
  How kind it was of him
To mind a slender man like me,
  He of the mighty limb!

"These to the printer," I exclaimed,
  And, in my humorous way,

I added, (as a trifling jest,)
    "There'll be the devil to pay."

He took the paper, and I watched,
    And saw him peep within;
At the first line he read, his face
    Was all upon the grin.

He read the next; the grin grew broad,
    And shot from ear to ear;
He read the third; a chuckling noise
    I now began to hear.

The fourth; he broke into a roar;
    The fifth; his waistband split;
The sixth; he burst five buttons off,
    And tumbled in a fit.

Ten days and nights, with sleepless eye,
    I watched that wretched man,
And since, I never dare to write
    As funny as I can.

Unsatisfied

"Only a housemaid!" She looked from the kitchen,—
    Neat was the kitchen and tidy was she;
There at her window a sempstress sat stitching;
    "Were I a sempstress, how happy I'd be!"

273

"Only a Queen!" She looked over the waters,—
    Fair was her kingdom and mighty was she;
There sat an Empress, with Queens for her daughters;
    "Were I an Empress, how happy I'd be!"

Still the old frailty they all of them trip in!
    Eve in her daughters is ever the same;
Give her all Eden, she sighs for a pippin;
    Give her an Empire, she pines for a name!

ANONYMOUS

(*1810-1860*)

Seven Negro Spirituals

My Lord, what a morning,[1]
My Lord, what a morning,
My Lord, what a morning,
  When the stars begin to fall!

You'll hear the trumpet sound
To wake the nations underground.
Looking to my God's right hand
  When the stars begin to fall!

My Lord, what a morning,
My Lord, what a morning,
My Lord, what a morning,
  When the stars begin to fall!

O, by an' by, by an' by,
I'm gwineter lay down my heavy load.

I know my robe's gwineter fit me well
(I'm gwineter lay down my heavy load).
I tried it on at de gates of hell.
(I'm gwinter lay down my heavy load.)

---

[1] Sometimes spelled "mourning."

O, Hell's a deep and dark despair
    (I'm gwineter lay down my heavy load).
O, stop, po' sinner, an' don't go dere.
    (I'm gwineter lay down my heavy load).

O, one of these mornin's bright an' fair
    (I'm gwineter lay down my heavy load.)
I'll put on my wings an' cleave de air.
    (I'm gwineter lay down my heavy load.)

Steal away, steal away, steal away to Jesus;
Steal away, steal away home,
I ain't got long to stay here.

My Lord, He calls me,
He calls me by the thunder,
The trumpet sounds within-a my soul;
I ain't got long to stay here.

Steal away, steal away, steal away to Jesus;
Steal away, steal away home,
I ain't got long to stay here.

Green trees a-bending,
Po' sinner stands a-trembling,
The trumpet sounds within-a my soul.
I ain't got long to stay here.

Steal away, steal away, steal away to Jesus;
Steal away, steal away home,
I ain't got long to stay here.

They crucified my Lord,
  And He never said a mumbaling word.
They crucified my Lord,
  And He never said a mumbaling word.
Not a word—not a word—not a word.

They nailed Him to the tree,
  And He never said a mumbaling word.
They nailed Him to the tree,
  And He never said a mumbaling word.
Not a word—not a word—not a word.

They pierced Him in the side,
  And He never said a mumbaling word.
They pierced Him in the side,
  And He never said a mumbaling word.
Not a word—not a word—not a word.

The blood came twinkaling down,
  And He never said a mumbaling word.
The blood came twinkaling down,
  And He never said a mumbaling word.
Not a word—not a word—not a word.

He bowed His head and died,
  And He never said a mumbaling word.

He bowed His head and died,
And He never said a mumbaling word.
Not a word—not a word—not a word.

Sometimes I feel like a motherless child,
Sometimes I feel like a motherless child,
Sometimes I feel like a motherless child,
A long ways from home.

Sometimes I feel like I'm almost gone,
Sometimes I feel like I'm almost gone,
Sometimes I feel like I'm almost gone,
A long ways from home.

Sometimes I feel like an eagle in the air,
Sometimes I feel like an eagle in the air,
Sometimes I feel like an eagle in the air,
A long ways from home.

Ezekiel saw the wheel
'Way up in the middle of the air;
Ezekiel saw the wheel
'Way in the middle of the air.
An' the little wheel runs by faith,
An' the big wheel runs by the grace of God—
Wheel in a wheel,
'Way in the middle of the air.

Some go to church for to sing an' shout,
　'Way up in the middle of the air;
Before six months they're all turned out,
　'Way in the middle of the air.

One of these days about twelve o'clock,
　'Way up in the middle of the air;
This whole world goin' to reel an' rock,
　'Way in the middle of the air.

Ezekiel saw the wheel
　'Way up in the middle of the air;
Ezekiel saw the wheel
　'Way in the middle of the air.
An' the little wheel runs by faith,
An' the big wheel runs by the grace of God—
Wheel in a wheel,
　'Way in the middle of the air.

I got a robe, you got a robe,
　All God's children got a robe.
When I get to heaven goin' to put on my robe,
　Goin' to shout all over God's heaven.

I got a crown, you got a crown,
　All God's children got a crown.
When I get to heaven goin' to put on my crown,
　Goin' to shine all over God's heaven.

279

I got a song, you got a song,
    All God's children got a song.
When I get to heaven goin' to sing out my song,
    Goin' to sing all over God's heaven.

JONES VERY

Enoch

I looked to find a man who walked with God,
Like the translated patriarch of old.
Though gladdened millions on his footstool trod,
Yet none with him did such sweet converse hold;
I heard the wind in low complaint go by,
That none its melodies like him could hear;
Day unto day spoke wisdom from on high,
Yet none with David turned a willing ear;
God walked alone unhonored through the earth;
For him no heart-built temple open stood,
The soul, forgetful of her nobler birth,
Had hewn him lofty shrines of stone and wood,
And left unfinished and in ruins still
The only temple he delights to fill.

The Spirit-Land

Father! thy wonders do not singly stand,
Nor far removed where feet have seldom strayed;
Around us ever lies the enchanted land,
In marvels rich to thine own sons displayed.
In finding thee are all things round us found;
In losing thee are all things lost beside;
Ears have we, but in vain strange voices sound;

And to our eyes the vision is denied.
We wander in the country far remote,
Mid tombs and ruined piles in death to dwell;
Or on the records of past greatness dote,
And for a buried soul the living sell;
While on our path bewildered falls the night
That ne'er returns us to the fields of light.

The Latter Rain

The latter rain,—it falls in anxious haste
Upon the sun-dried fields and branches bare,
Loosening with searching drops the rigid waste
As if it would each root's lost strength repair;
But not a blade grows green as in the spring;
No swelling twig puts forth its thickening leaves;
The robins only mid the harvests sing,
Pecking the grain that scatters from the sheaves;
The rain falls still,—the fruit all ripened drops,
It pierces chestnut-burr and walnut-shell;
The furrowed fields disclose the yellow crops;
Each bursting pod of talents used can tell;
And all that once received the early rain
Declare to man it was not sent in vain.

Nature

The bubbling brook doth leap when I come by,
Because my feet find measure with its call;
The birds know when the friend they love is nigh,

For I am known to them, both great and small.
The flower that on the lonely hill-side grows
Expects me there when Spring its bloom has given;
And many a tree and bush my wanderings knows,
And e'en the clouds and silent stars of heaven;
For he who with his Maker walks aright,
Shall be their lord as Adam was before;
His ear shall catch each sound with new delight,
Each object wear the dress that then it wore;
And he, as when erect in soul he stood,
Hear from his Father's lips that all is good.

Day

Day! I lament that none can hymn thy praise
In fitting strains, of all thy riches bless;
Though thousands sport them in thy golden rays,
Yet none like thee their Maker's name confess.
Great fellow of my being! woke with me,
Thou dost put on thy dazzling robes of light,
And onward from the east go forth to free
Thy children from the bondage of the night.
I hail thee, pilgrim, on thy lonely way,
Whose look on all alike benignant shine;
A child of light, like these, I cannot stay,
But on the world I bless must soon decline,
New rising still, though setting to mankind,
And ever in the eternal west my dayspring find.

The Wind-Flower

Thou lookest up with meek, confiding eye
Upon the clouded smile of April's face,
Unharm'd though Winter stands uncertain by,
Eyeing with jealous glance each opening grace.
Thou trustest wisely! in thy faith array'd,
More glorious thou than Israel's wisest king.
Such faith was His whom men to death betray'd,
As thine who hearest the timid voice of Spring,
While other flowers still hide them from her call
Along the river's brink and meadow bare.
Thee will I seek beside the stony wall,
And in thy trust with childlike heart would share,
O'erjoyed that in thy early leaves I find
A lesson taught by Him who loved all humankind.

Morning

The light will never open sightless eyes,
It comes to those who willingly would see;
And every object—hill, and stream, and skies,
Rejoice within the encircling line to be.
'Tis day—the field is fill'd with busy hands,
The shop resounds with noisy workmen's din,
The traveller with his staff already stands
His yet unmeasured journey to begin.
The light breaks gently, too, within the breast,
Yet there no eye awaits the crimson morn,

The forge and noisy anvil are at rest,
Nor men nor oxen tread the fields of corn,
Nor pilgrim lifts his staff—it is not day
To those who find on earth their place to stay.

The Tree

I love thee when thy swelling buds appear,
And one by one their tender leaves unfold,
As if they knew that warmer suns were near,
Nor longer sought to hide from winter's cold;
And when with darker growth thy leaves are seen
To veil from view the early robin's nest,
I love to lie beneath thy waving screen,
With limbs by summer's heat and toil oppress'd;
And when the autumn winds have stript thee bare,
And round thee lies the smooth, untrodden snow,
When naught is thine that made thee once so fair,
I love to watch thy shadowy form below,
And through thy leafless arms to look above
On stars that brighter beam when most we need their love.

October

The frost is out, and in the open fields,
And late within the woods, I marked his track
The unwary flower his icy finger feels.
And at their touch the crispéd leaf rolls back;
Look how the mape o'er a sea of green
Waves in the autumnal wind his flag of red!

285

First struck of all the forest's spreading screen,
Most beauteous, too, the earliest of her dead.
Go on: thy task is kindly meant by Him
Whose is each flower and richly covered bough;
And though the leaves hang dead on every limb,
Still will I praise His love, that early now
Has sent before this herald of decay
To bid me heed before the approach of winter's sterner day.

The Robin

Thou need'st not flutter from thy half-built nest,
Whene'er thou hear'st man's hurrying feet go by,
Fearing his eye for harm may on thee rest,
Or he thy young unfinished cottage spy;
All will not heed thee on that swinging bough,
Nor care that round thy shelter spring the leaves,
Nor watch thee on the pool's wet margin now,
For clay to plaster straws thy cunning weaves;
All will not hear thy sweet outpouring joy,
That with morn's stillness blends the voice of song,
For over-anxious cares their souls employ,
That else upon thy music borne along
And the light wings of heart-ascending prayer
Had learned that Heaven is pleased thy simple joys to share.

The New World

The night that has no star lit up by God,
The day that round men shines who still are blind,
The earth their grave-turned feet for ages trod,

286

And sea swept over by His mighty wind—
All these have passed away, the melting dream
That flitted o'er the sleeper's half-shut eye,
When touched by morning's golden-darting beam;
And he beholds around the earth and sky
That ever real stands, the rolling shores
And heaving billows of the boundless main,
That show, though time is past, no trace of years.
And earth restored he sees as his again,
The earth that fades not and the heavens that stand,
Their strong foundations laid and held by God's right hand.

The Dead

I see them—crowd on crowd they walk the earth,
Dry leafless trees no autumn wind laid bare;
And in their nakedness find cause for mirth,
And all unclad would winter's rudeness dare;
No sap doth through their clattering branches flow,
Whence springing leaves and blossoms bright appear;
Their hearts the living God have ceased to know
Who gives the springtime to the expectant year.
They mimic life, as if from Him to steal
His glow of health to paint the livid cheek;
They borrow words for thoughts they cannot feel,
That with a seeming heart their tongue may speak;
And in their show of life more dead they live
Than those that to the earth with many tears they give.

JOHN GODFREY SAXE

(1816-1887)

The Blind Men and the Elephant

A Hindoo Fable

It was six men of Indostan
　　To learning much inclined,
Who went to see the Elephant
　　(Though all of them were blind),
That each by observation
　　Might satisfy his mind.

The *First* approached the Elephant,
　　And happening to fall
Against his broad and sturdy side,
　　At once began to bawl:
"God bless me! but the Elephant
　　Is very like a wall!"

The *Second*, feeling of the tusk,
　　Cried, "Ho! what have we here
So very round and smooth and sharp?
　　To me 'tis mighty clear
This wonder of an Elephant
　　Is very like a spear!"

The *Third* approached the animal,
　　And happening to take

The squirming trunk within his hands,
  Thus boldly up and spake:
"I see," quoth he, "the Elephant
  Is very like a snake!"

The *Fourth* reached out an eager hand,
  And felt about the knee.
"What most this wondrous beast is like
  Is mighty plain," quoth he;
" 'Tis clear enough the Elephant
  Is very like a tree!"

The *Fifth* who chanced to touch the ear,
  Said: "E'en the blindest man
Can tell what this resembles most;
  Deny the fact who can,
This marvel of an Elephant
  Is very like a fan!"

The *Sixth* no sooner had begun
  About the beast to grope,
Than, seizing on the swinging tail
  That fell within his scope,
"I see," quoth he, "the Elephant
  Is very like a rope!"

And so these men of Indostan
  Disputed loud and long,
Each in his own opinion
  Exceeding stiff and strong,
Though each was partly in the right,
  And all were in the wrong!

The Moral:
So oft in theologic wars,
    The disputants, I ween,
Rail on in utter ignorance
    Of what each other mean,
And prate about an Elephant
    Not one of them has seen!

My Familiar

Again I hear that creaking step—
    He's rapping at the door!
Too well I know the boding sound
    That ushers in a bore.
I do not tremble when I meet
    The stoutest of my foes,
But Heaven defend me from the friend
    Who comes—but never goes!

He drops into my easy-chair,
    And asks about the news;
He peers into my manuscript,
    And gives his candid views;
He tells me where he likes the line,
    And where he's forced to grieve;
He takes the strangest liberties—
    But never takes his leave.

He reads my daily paper through
    Before I've seen a word;

He scans the lyric that I wrote
  And thinks it quite absurd;
He calmly smokes my last cigar,
  And coolly asks for more;
He opens everything he sees—
  Except the entry door!

He talks about his fragile health,
  And tells me of the pains
He suffers from a score of ills
  Of which he ne'er complains;
And how he struggled once with death
  To keep the fiend at bay;
On themes like those away he goes—
  But never goes away!

He tells me of the carping words
  Some shallow critic wrote;
And every precious paragraph
  Familiarly can quote;
He thinks the writer did me wrong;
  He'd like to run him through!
He says a thousand pleasant things—
  But never says "Adieu!"

Whene'er he comes, that dreadful man,
  Disguise it as I may,
I know that, like an Autumn rain,
  He'll last throughout the day.
In vain I speak of urgent tasks;
  In vain I scowl and pout;

A frown is no extinguisher—
   It does not put him out!

I mean to take the knocker off,
   Put crape upon the door,
Or hint to John that I am gone
   To stay a month or more.
I do not tremble when I meet
   The stoutest of my foes,
But Heaven defend me from the friend
   Who never, never goes!

Early Rising

God bless the man who first invented sleep!"
   So Sancho Panza said, and so say I:
And bless him, also, that he didn't keep
   His great discovery to himself; nor try
To make it—as the lucky fellow might—
A close monopoly by patent-right!

Yes—bless the man who first invented sleep,
   (I really can't avoid the iteration;)
But blast the man, with curses loud and deep,
   Whate'er the rascal's name, or age, or station,
Who first invented, and went round advising,
That artificial cut-off—Early Rising!

"Rise with the lark, and with the lark to bed,"
   Observes some solemn, sentimental owl;

Maxims like these are very cheaply said;
   But, ere you make yourself a fool or fowl,
Pray just inquire about his rise and fall,
And whether larks have any beds at all!

The time for honest folks to be a-bed
   Is in the morning, if I reason right;
And he who cannot keep his precious head
   Upon his pillow till it's fairly light,
And so enjoy his forty morning winks,
Is up to knavery; or else—he drinks!

Thompson, who sang about the "Seasons," said
   It was a glorious thing to *rise* in season;
But then he said it—lying—in his bed,
   At ten o'clock A.M.,—the very reason
He wrote so charmingly. The simple fact is
His preaching wasn't sanctioned by his practice.

'Tis, doubtless, well to be sometimes awake,—
   Awake to duty, and awake to truth,—
But when, alas! a nice review we take
   Of our best deeds and days, we find, in sooth,
The hours that leave the slightest cause to weep
Are those we passed in childhood or asleep!

'Tis beautiful to leave the world awhile
   For the soft visions of the gentle night;
And free, at last, from mortal care or guile,
   To live as only in the angel's sight,
In sleep's sweet realm so cosily shut in,
Where, at the worst, we only *dream* of sin!

So let us sleep, and give the Maker praise.
   I like the lad who, when his father thought
To clip his morning nap by hackneyed phrase
   Of vagrant worm by early songster caught,
Cried, "Served him right!—it's not at all surprising;
The worm was punished, sir, for early rising!"

HENRY DAVID THOREAU

(*1817-1862*)

Independence

My life more civil is and free
Than any civil polity.

Ye princes, keep your realms
     And circumscribèd power,
Not wide as are my dreams,
     Nor rich as is this hour.

What can ye give which I have not?
What can ye take which I have got?
     Can ye defend the dangerless?
     Can ye inherit nakedness?

To all true wants Time's ear is deaf,
Penurious States lend no relief
          Out of their pelf:
     But a free soul—thank God—
          Can help itself.

     Be sure your fate
Doth keep apart its state,—
Not linked with any band,
Even the noblest in the land,—

In tented fields with cloth of gold
     No place doth hold,

But is more chivalrous than they are,
    And sigheth for a nobler war;

A finer strain its trumpet rings,
    A brighter gleam its armor flings.

The life that I aspire to live,
    No man proposeth me;
No trade upon the street
    Wears its emblazonry.

Smoke

Light-wingèd Smoke! Icarian bird,
Melting thy pinions in thy upward flight;
Lark without song, and messenger of dawn,
Circling above the hamlets as thy nest;
Or else, departing dream, and shadowy form
Of midnight vision, gathering up thy skirts;
    By night star-veiling, and by day
Darkening the light and blotting out the sun;
Go thou, my incense, upward from this hearth,
And ask the gods to pardon this clear flame.

Mist

Low-anchored cloud,
Newfoundland air,
Fountain-head and source of rivers,
Dew-cloth, dream-drapery,

And napkin spread by fays;
Drifting meadow of the air,
Where bloom the daisied banks and violets,
And in whose fenny labyrinth
The bittern booms and heron wades;
Spirit of lakes and seas and rivers,—
Bear only perfumes and the scent
Of healing herbs to just men's fields.

Haze

Woof of the sun, ethereal gauze,
Woven of Nature's richest stuffs,
Visible heat, air-water, and dry sea,
Last conquest of the eye;
Toil of the day displayed, sun-dust,
Aerial surf upon the shores of earth,
Ethereal estuary, frith of light,
Breakers of air, billows of heat,
Fine summer spray on inland seas;
Bird of the sun, transparent-winged
Owlet of noon, soft-pinioned,
From hearth or stubble rising without song;
Establish thy serenity o'er the fields.

All Things Are Current Found

All things are current found
On earthly ground,
Spirits and elements
Have their descents.

297

Night and day, year on year,
High and low, far and near,
These are our own aspects,
These are our own regrets.

Ye gods of the shore,
Who abide evermore,
I see your far headland,
Stretching on either hand;

I hear the sweet evening sounds
From your undecaying grounds;
Cheat me no more with time,
Take me to your clime.

Summer Rain

My books I'd fain cast off, I cannot read,
'Twixt every page my thoughts go stray at large
Down in the meadow, where is richer feed,
And will not mind to hit their proper targe.

Plutarch was good, and so was Homer, too;
Our Shakespeare's life were rich to live again;
What Plutarch read, that was not good nor true,
Nor Shakespeare's books, unless his books were men.

Here while I lie beneath this walnut bough,
What care I for the Greeks or for Troy town,
If juster battles are enacted now
Between the ants upon this hummock's crown?

Bid Homer wait till I the issue learn,
If red or black the gods will favor most,
Or yonder Ajax will the phalanx turn,
Struggling to heave some rock against the host.

Tell Shakespeare to attend some leisure hour,
For now I've business with this drop of dew,
And see you not, the clouds prepare a shower—
I'll meet him shortly when the sky is blue.

This bed of herd's-grass and wild oats was spread
Last year with nicer skill than monarchs use,
A clover tuft is pillow for my head,
And violets quite overtop my shoes.

And now the cordial clouds have shut all in,
And gently swells the wind to say all's well,
The scattered drops are falling fast and thin,
Some in the pool, some in the flower-bell.

I am well drenched upon my bed of oats;
But see that globe come rolling down its stem,
Now like a lonely planet there it floats,
And now it sinks into my garment's hem.

Drip drip the trees for all the country round,
And richness rare distils from every bough;
The wind alone it is makes every sound,
Shaking down crystals on the leaves below.

For shame the sun will never show himself,
Who could not with his beams e'er melt me so,

My dripping locks—they would become an elf,
Who in a bearded coat does gayly go.

Men Say They Know Many Things

Men say they know many things;
But lo! they have taken wings—
The arts and sciences,
And a thousand appliances;
The wind that blows
Is all that any body knows.

Love

Let such pure hate still underprop
Our love, that we may be
Each other's conscience,
And have our sympathy
Mainly from thence.

We'll one another treat like gods,
And all the faith we have
In virtue and in truth, bestow
On either, and suspicion leave
To gods below.

Two solitary stars—
Unmeasured systems far
Between us roll,
But by our conscious light we are
Determined to one pole.

What need confound the sphere—
Love can afford to wait,
For it no hour's too late
That witnesseth one duty's end,
Or to another doth beginning lend.

Conscience

Conscience is instinct bred in the house
Feeling and Thinking propagate the sin
By an unnatural breeding in and in.
I say, turn it out doors,
Into the moors.
I love a life whose plot is simple,
And does not thicken with every pimple,
A soul so sound no sickly conscience binds it,
That makes the universe no worse than't finds it.

I love an earnest soul,
Whose mighty joy and sorrow
Are not drowned in a bowl,
And brought to life tomorrow;
That lives one tragedy,
And not seventy;
A conscience worth keeping,
Laughing not weeping;
A conscience wise and steady,
And forever ready;
Not changing with events,
Dealing in compliments;

A conscience exercised about
Large things, where one *may* doubt.

I love a soul not all of wood,
Predestinated to be good,
But true to the backbone
Unto itself alone,
And false to none;
Born to its own affairs,
Its own joys and own cares;
By whom the work which God begun
Is finished, and not undone;
Taken up where he left off,
Whether to worship or to scoff;
If not good, why then evil,
If not good god, good devil.

Goodness! you hypocrite, come out of that,
Live your life, do your work, then take your hat.
I have no patience towards
Such conscientious cowards.
Give me simple laboring folk,
Who love their work,
Whose virtue is a song
To cheer God along.

WILLIAM ELLERY CHANNING, II

(1818-1901)

Hymn of the Earth

My highway is unfeatured air,
My consorts are the sleepless stars,
And men my giant arms upbear,
My arms unstained and free from scars.

I rest forever on my way,
Rolling around the happy Sun;
My children love the sunny day,
But noon and night to me are one.

My heart has pulses like their own,
I am their mother, and my veins,
Though built of the enduring stone,
Thrill as do theirs with godlike pains.

The forests and the mountains high,
The foaming ocean and the springs,
The plains—O pleasant Company,
My voice through all your anthem rings.

Ye are so cheerful in your minds,
Content to smile, content to share:
My being in your chorus finds
The echo of the spheral air.

No leaf may fall, no pebble roll,
No drop of water lose the road;
The issues of the general Soul
Are mirrored in its round abode.

The Earth-Spirit

I have woven shrouds of air
    In a loom of hurrying light,
For the trees which blossoms bear,
    And gilded them with sheets of bright;
I fall upon the grass like love's first kiss;
I make the golden flies and their fine bliss,
I paint the hedgerows in the lane,
And clover white and red the pathways bear;
I laugh aloud in sudden gusts of rain
To see the ocean lash himself in air;
I throw smooth shells and weeds along the beach,
And pour the curling waves far o'er the glossy reach;
Swing birds' nests in the elms, and shake cool moss
Along the aged beams, and hide their loss,
The very broad rough stones I gladden too;
Some willing seeds I drop along their sides,
Nourish the generous plant with freshening dew,
Till there where all was waste, true joy abides.
The peaks of aged mountains, with my care
Smile in the red of glowing morn elate;
I bind the caverns of the sea with hair,
Glossy, and long, and rich as kings' estate;
I polish the green ice, and gleam the wall
With the white frost, and leaf the brown trees tall.

And Here the Hermit Sat

And here the hermit sat, and told his beads,
And stroked his flowing locks, red as the fire,
Summed up his tale of moon and sun and star:
"How blest are we," he deemed, "who so comprise
The essence of the whole, and of ourselves,
As in a Venice flask of lucent shape,
Ornate of gilt Arabic, and inscribed
With Suras from Time's Koran, live and pray,
More than half grateful for the glittering prize,
Human existence! If I note my powers,
So poor and frail a toy, the insect's prey,
Itched by a berry, festered by a plum,
The very air infecting my thin frame
With its malarial trick, whom every day
Rushes upon and hustles to the grave,
Yet raised, by the great love that broods o'er all
Responsive, to a height beyond all thought."

He ended, as the nightly prayer and fast
Summoned him inward. But I sat and heard
The night-hawks rip the air above my head,
Till midnight o'er the warm, dry, dewless rocks;
And saw the blazing dog-star droop his fire,
And the low comet, trailing to the south,
Bend his reverted gaze, and leave us free.

JAMES RUSSELL LOWELL

(*1819-1891*)

The Courtin'

(*From "The Biglow Papers"*)

God makes sech nights, all white an' still
  Fur'z you can look or listen,
Moonshine an' snow on field an' hill,
  All silence an' all glisten.

Zekle crep' up quite unbeknown
  An' peeked in thru' the winder,
An' there sot Huldy all alone,
  'Ith no one nigh to hender.

A fireplace filled the room's one side
  With half a cord o' wood in—
There warn't no stoves (tell comfort died)
  To bake ye to a puddin'.

The wa'nut logs shot sparkles out
  Towards the pootiest, bless her,
An' leetle flames danced all about
  The chiny on the dresser.

Agin the chimbley crook-necks hung,
  An' in amongst 'em rusted
The ole queen's arm thet gran'ther Young
  Fetched back from Concord busted.

The very room, coz she was in,
   Seemed warm from floor to ceilin',
An' she looked full ez rosy agin
   Ez the apples she was peelin'.

'Twas kin' o' kingdom-come to look
   On sech a blessed cretur,
A dogrose blushin' to a brook
   Ain't modester nor sweeter.

He was six foot o' man, A 1,
   Clear grit an' human natur';
None couldn't quicker pitch a ton
   Nor dror a furrer straighter.

He'd sparked it with full twenty gals,
   He'd squired 'em, danced 'em, druv 'em,
Fust this one, an' then thet, by spells—
   All is, he couldn't love 'em.

But long o' her his veins 'ould run
   All crinkly like curled maple,
The side she breshed felt full o' sun
   Ez a south slope in Ap'il.

She thought no v'ice hed sech a swing
   Ez hisn in the choir;
My! when he made Ole Hundred ring
   She *knowed* the Lord was nigher.

An' she'd blush scarlit, right in prayer,
   When her new meetin'-bunnet

Felt somehow thru' its crown a pair
 O blue eyes sot upun it.

Thet night, I tell ye, she looked *some*!
 She seemed to've gut a new soul,
For she felt sartin-sure he'd come,
 Down to her very shoe-sole.

She heered a foot, an' knowed it tu,
 A-raspin' on the scraper,—
All ways to once her feelin's flew
 Like sparks in burnt-up paper.

He kin' o' l'itered on the mat
 Some doubtfle o' the sekle,
His heart kep' goin' pity-pat,
 But hern went pity Zekle.

An' yit she gin her cheer a jerk
 Ez though she wished him furder,
An' on her apples kep' to work,
 Parin' away like murder.

"You want to see my Pa, I s'pose!"
 "Wal . . . no . . . I come designin' "—
"To see my Ma? She's sprinklin' clo'es
 Agin tomorrer's i'nin'."

To say why gals act so or so,
 Or don't, 'ould be presumin';
Mebby to mean *yes* an' say *no*
 Comes nateral to women.

He stood a spell on one foot fust,
  Then stood a spell on t'other,
An' on which one he felt the wust
  He couldn't ha' told ye nuther.

Says he, "I'd better call agin";
  Says she, "Think likely, Mister":
Thet last word pricked him like a pin,
  An' . . . Wal, he up an' kist her.

When Ma bimeby upon 'em slips,
  Huldy sot pale ez ashes,
All kin' o' smily roun' the lips
  An' teary roun' the lashes.

For she was jes' the quiet kind
  Whose naturs never vary,
Like streams that keep a summer mind
  Snowhid in Jenooary.

The blood clost roun' her heart felt glued
  Too tight for all expressin',
Tell mother see how metters stood,
  An' gin 'em both her blessin'.

Then her red come back like the tide
  Down to the Bay o' Fundy,
An' all I know is they was cried
  In meetin' come nex' Sunday.

To a Recruiting Sergeant

(From "The Biglow Papers")

Thrash away, you'll *hev* to rattle
    On them kittle-drums o' yourn,—
'Taint a knowin' kind o' cattle
    Thet is ketched with moldy corn;
Put in stiff, you fifer feller,
    Let folks see how spry you be,—
Guess you'll toot till you are yeller
    'Fore you git ahold o' me!

Thet air flag's a leetle rotten,
    Hope it ain't your Sunday's best;—
Fact! it takes a sight o' cotton
    To stuff out a soger's chest:
Sence we farmers hev to pay fer't,
    Ef you must wear humps like these,
Sposin' you should try salt hay fer't,
    It would du ez slick ez grease.

'Twouldn't suit them Southun fellers,
    They're a dreffle graspin' set,
We must ollers blow the bellers
    Wen they want their irons het;
May be it's all right ez preachin',
    But *my* narves it kind o' grates,
Wen I see the overreachin'
    O' them nigger-drivin' States.

Them thet rule us, them slave-traders,
  Haint they cut a thunderin' swarth,
(Helped by Yankee renegaders),
  Thru the vartu o' the North!
We begin to think it's nater
  To take sarse an' not be riled;—
Who'd expect to see a tater
  All on eend at bein' biled?

Ez fer war, I call it murder,—
  There you hev it plain an' flat;
I don't want to go no furder
  Than my Testyment fer that;
God hez sed so plump an' fairly,
  It's ez long ez it is broad,
An' you've gut to git up airly
  Ef you want to take in God.

'Taint your eppyletts an' feathers
  Make the thing a grain more right;
'Taint afollerin' your bell-wethers
  Will excuse ye in His sight;
Ef you take a sword an' dror it,
  An' go stick a feller thru,
Guv'ment aint to answer for it,
  God'll send the bill to you.

Wut's the use o' meetin'-goin'
  Every Sabbath, wet or dry,
Ef it's right to go amowin'
  Feller-men like oats an' rye?

I dunno but wut it's pooty
   Trainin' round in bobtail coats,—
But it's curus Christian dooty
   This 'ere cuttin' folks's throats.

They may talk o' Freedom's airy[1]
   Tell they're pupple in the face,—
It's a grand gret cemetary
   Fer the barthrights of our race;
They jest want this Californy
   So's to lug new slave-states in
To abuse ye, an' to scorn ye,
   An' to plunder ye like sin.

Aint it cute to see a Yankee
   Take sech everlastin' pains,
All to git the Devil's thankee,
   Helpin' on 'em weld their chains?
Wy, it's jest ez clear ez figgers,
   Clear ez one an' one make two,
Chaps thet make black slaves o' niggers
   Want to make wite slaves o' you.

Tell ye jest the eend I've come to
   Arter cipherin' plaguy smart,
An' it makes a handy sum, tu,
   Any gump could larn by heart;
Laborin' man an' laborin' woman
   Hev one glory an' one shame,
Ev'y thin' thet's done inhuman
   Injers all on 'em the same.

[1] area.

312

'Taint by turnin' out to hack folks
    You're agoin' to git your right,
Nor by lookin' down on black folks
    Coz you're put upon by wite;
Slavery aint o' nary color,
    'Taint the hide thet makes it wus,
All it keers fer in a feller
    'S jest to make him fill its pus.

Want to tackle *me* in, du ye?
    I expect you'll hev to wait;
Wen cold lead puts daylight thru ye
    You'll begin to kal'late;
'Spose the crows wun't fall to pickin'
    All the carkiss from your bones,
Coz you helped to give a lickin'
    To them poor half-Spanish drones?

Jest go home an' ask our Nancy
    Wether I'd be sech a goose
Ez to jine ye,—guess you'd fancy
    The etarnal bung was loose!
She wants me fer home consumption,
    Let alone the hay's to mow,—
Ef you're arter folks o' gumption,
    You've a darned long row to hoe.

Take them editors thet's crowin'
    Like a cockerel three months old,—
Don't ketch any on 'em goin',
    Though they *be* so blasted bold;

313

Aint they a prime lot o' fellers?
　'Fore they think on't guess they'll sprout,
(Like a peach thet's got the yellers)
　With the meanness bustin' out.

Wal, go 'long to help 'em stealin'
　Bigger pens to cram with slaves,
Help the men thet's ollers dealin'
　Insults on your fathers' graves;
Help the strong to grind the feeble,
　Help the many agin the few,
Help the men thet call your people
　Witewashed slaves an' peddlin' crew!

Massachusetts, God forgive her,
　She's akneelin' with the rest,
She thet ough' to ha' clung ferever
　In her grand old eagle-nest;
She thet ough' to stand so fearless
　Wile the wracks are round her hurled,
Holdin' up a beacon peerless
　To the oppressed of all the world!

Ha'n't they sold your colored seamen?
　Ha'n't they made your env'ys w'iz?
Wut'll make ye act like free men?
　Wut'll git your dander riz?
Come, I'll tell ye wut I'm thinkin'
　Is our dooty in this fix,
They'd ha' done 't ez quick ez winkin'
　In the days o' seventy-six.

Clang the bells in every steeple,
  Call all true men to disown
The tradoocers of our people,
  The enslavers o' their own;
Let our dear old Bay State proudly
  Put the trumpet to her mouth,
Let her ring this messidge loudly
  In the ears of all the South:

"I'll return ye good for evil
  Much ez we frail mortils can,
But I won't go help the Devil
  Makin' man the cus o' man;
Call me coward, call me traiter,
  Jest ez suits your mean idees,—
Here I stand a tyrant-hater,
  An' the friend o' God an' Peace!"

Ef I'd *my* way I hed ruther
  We should go to work an' part,—
They take one way, we take t'other,—
  Guess it wouldn't break my heart;
Man hed ough' to put asunder
  Them thet God has noways jined;
An' I shouldn't gretly wonder
  Ef there's thousands o' my mind.

The Pious Editor's Creed

(From "The Biglow Papers")

I du believe in Freedom's cause,
    Ez fur away ez Payris is;
I love to see her stick her claws
    In them infarnal Phayrisees;
It's wal enough agin a king
    To dror resolves an' triggers,—
But libbaty's a kind o' thing
    Thet don't agree with niggers.

I du believe the people want
    A tax on teas an' coffees,
Thet nothin' aint extravygunt,—
    Purvidin' I'm in office;
Fer I hev loved my country sence
    My eye-teeth filled their sockets,
An' Uncle Sam I reverence,
    Partic'larly his pockets.

I du believe in *any* plan
    O' levyin' the taxes,
Ez long ez, like a lumberman,
    I git jest wut I axes:
I go free-trade thru thick an' thin,
    Because it kind o' rouses
The folks to vote,—an' keeps us in
    Our quiet custom-houses.

I du believe it's wise an' good
    To sen' out furrin missions,
Thet is, on sartin understood
    An' orthydox conditions;—
I mean nine thousan' dolls. per ann.,
    Nine thousan' more fer outfit,
An' me to recommend a man
    The place 'ould jest about fit.

I du believe in special ways
    O' prayin' an' convartin';
The bread comes back in many days,
    An' buttered, tu, fer sartin;
I mean in prayin' till one busts
    On wut the party chooses,
An' in convartin' public trusts
    To very privit uses.

I du believe hard coin the stuff
    Fer 'lectioneers to spout on;
The people's ollers soft enough
    To make hard money out on;
Dear Uncle Sam pervides fer his,
    An' gives a good-sized junk to all,—
I don't care *how* hard money is,
    Ez long ez mine's paid punctooal.

I du believe with all my soul
    In the gret Press's freedom,
To pint the people to the goal
    An' in the traces lead 'em;

Palsied the arm thet forges yokes
    At my fat contracts squintin',
An' withered be the nose thet pokes
    Inter the gov'ment printin'!

I du believe thet I should give
    Wut's his'n unto Cæsar,
Fer it's by him I move an' live,
    Frum him by bread an' cheese air;
I du believe thet all o' me
    Doth bear his superscription,—
Will, conscience, honor, honesty,
    An' things o' thet description.

I du believe in prayer an' praise
    To him that hez the grantin'
O' jobs,—in every thin' thet pays,
    But most of all in CANTIN';
This doth my cup with marcies fill,
    This lays all thought o' sin to rest,—
I *don't* believe in princerple,
    But O, I *du* in interest.

I du believe in bein' this
    Or thet, ez it may happen
One way or t'other hendiest is
    To ketch the people nappin';
It aint by princerples nor men
    My preudunt course is steadied,—
I scent which pays the best, an' then
    Go into it baldheaded.

I du believe thet holdin' slaves
    Comes nat'ral tu a Presidunt,
Let 'lone the rowdedow it saves
    To hev a wal-broke precedunt;
Fer any office, small or gret,
    I couldn't ax with no face,
Without I'd ben, thru dry an' wet,
    Th' unrizzest kind o' doughface.

I du believe wutever trash
    'll keep the people in blindness,—
Thet we the Mexicuns can thrash
    Right inter brotherly kindness,
Thet bombshells, grape, an' powder 'n' ball
    Air good-will's strongest magnets,
Thet peace, to make it stick at all,
    Must be druv in with bagnets.

In short, I firmly du believe
    In Humbug generally,
Fer it's a thing thet I perceive
    To hev a solid vally;
This heth my faithful shepherd ben,
    In pasturs sweet heth led me,
An' this'll keep the people green
    To feed ez they hev fed me.

What Mr. Robinson Thinks

(*From "The Biglow Papers"*)

Guvener B, is a sensible man;
 He stays to his home an' looks arter his folks;
He draws his furrer ez straight ez he can,
 An' into nobody's tater-patch pokes;
   But John P.
   Robinson he
  Sez he wunt vote fer Guvener B.

My! aint it terrible? Wut shall we du?
 We can't never choose him o' course,—thet's flat;
Guess we shall hev to come round (don't you?)
 An' go in fer thunder an' guns, an' all that;
   Fer John P.
   Robinson he
  Sez he wunt vote fer Guvener B.

Gineral C. is a dreffle smart man:
 He's ben on all sides thet give places or pelf;
But consistency still wuz a part of his plan,—
 He's been true to *one* party,—an' thet is himself;—
   So John P.
   Robinson he
  Sez he shall vote fer Gineral C.

Gineral C. he goes in fer the war;
 He don't vally princerple more'n an old cud;
Wut did God make us raytional creeturs fer,

But glory an' gunpowder, plunder an' blood?
    So John P.
    Robinson he
Sez he shall vote fer Gineral C.

We were gittin' on nicely up here to our village,
  With good old idees o' wut's right an' wut aint,
We kind o' thought Christ went agin war an' pillage,
  An' thet eppyletts worn't the best mark of a saint;
    But John P.
    Robinson he
Sez this kind o' thing's an exploded idee.

The side of our country must ollers be took,
  An' President Polk, you know, *he* is our country,
An' the angel thet writes all our sins in a book
  Puts the *debit* to him, an' to us the *per contry*
    An' John P.
    Robinson he
Sez this is his view o' the thing to a T.

Parson Wilbur he calls all these argimunts lies;
  Sez they're nothin' on airth but jest *fee, faw, fum;*
An' thet all this big talk of our destinies
  Is half on it ign'ance, an' t'other half rum;
    But John P.
    Robinson he
Sez it aint no sech thing; an', of course, so must we.

Parson Wilbur sez *he* never heerd in his life
  Thet th' Apostles rigged out in their swaller-tail coats,

321

An' marched round in front of a drum an' a fife,
  To git some on 'em office, an' some on 'em votes;
      But John P.
      Robinson he
  Sez they didn't know everythin' down in Judee.

Wal, it's a marcy we've gut folks to tell us
  The rights an' the wrongs o' these matters, I vow,—
God sends country lawyers, an' other wise fellers,
  To start the world's team wen it gits in a slough;
      Fer John P.
      Robinson he
  Sez the world'll go right, ef he hollers out Gee!

Prelude

(From "The Vision of Sir Launfal")

Over his keys the musing organist,
  Beginning doubtfully and far away,
First lets his fingers wander as they list,
  And builds a bridge from Dreamland for his lay:
Then, as the touch of his loved instrument
  Gives hope and fervor, nearer draws his theme,
First guessed by faint auroral flushes sent
  Along the wavering vista of his dream.

Not only around our infancy
  Doth heaven with all its splendors lie;
Daily, with souls that cringe and plot,
  We Sinais climb and know it not.

Over our manhood bend the skies;
  Against our fallen and traitor lives
The great winds utter prophecies;
  With our faint hearts the mountain strives;
Its arms outstretched, the druid wood
  Waits with its benedicite;
And to our age's drowsy blood
  Still shouts the inspiring sea.
Earth gets its price for what Earth gives us;
  The beggar is taxed for a corner to die in,
The priest hath his fee who comes and shrives us,
  We bargain for the graves we lie in;
At the devil's booth are all things sold,
Each ounce of dross costs its ounce of gold;
  For a cap and bells our lives we pay,
Bubbles we buy with a whole soul's tasking:
  'Tis heaven alone that is given away,
'Tis only God may be had for the asking;
No price is set on the lavish summer;
June may be had by the poorest comer.

And what is so rare as a day in June?
  Then, if ever, come perfect days;
Then Heaven tries earth if it be in tune,
  And over it softly her warm ear lays:
Whether we look, or whether we listen,
We hear life murmur, or see it glisten;
Every clod feels a stir of might,
  An instinct within it that reaches and towers,
And, groping blindly above it for light,
  Climbs to a soul in grass and flowers;
The flush of life may well be seen

323

Thrilling back over hills and valleys;
The cowslip startles in meadows green,
The buttercup catches the sun in its chalice,
And there's never a leaf nor a blade too mean
To be some happy creature's palace;
The little bird sits at his door in the sun,
Atilt like a blossom among the leaves,
And lets his illumined being o'errun
With the deluge of summer it receives;
His mate feels the eggs beneath her wings,
And the heart in her dumb breast flutters and sings;
He sings to the wide world, and she to her nest,—
In the nice ear of Nature which song is the best?

Now is the high-tide of the year,
And whatever of life hath ebbed away
Comes flooding back with a ripply cheer,
Into every bare inlet and creek and bay;
Now the heart is so full that a drop overfills it,
We are happy now because God wills it;
No matter how barren the past may have been,
'Tis enough for us now that the leaves are green;
We sit in the warm shade and feel right well
How the sap creeps up and the blossoms swell;
We may shut our eyes but we cannot help knowing
That skies are clear and grass is growing;
The breeze comes whispering in our ear,
That dandelions are blossoming near,
That maize has sprouted, that streams are flowing,
That the river is bluer than the sky,
That the robin is plastering his house hard by;

And if the breeze kept the good news back,
For other couriers we should not lack;
   We could guess it all by yon heifer's lowing,—
And hark! how clear bold chanticleer,
Warmed with the new wine of the year,
   Tells all in his lusty crowing!

Joy comes, grief goes, we know not how;
Everything is happy now,
   Everything is upward striving;
'Tis as easy now for the heart to be true
As for grass to be green or skies to be blue,—
   'Tis the natural way of living:
Who knows whither the clouds have fled?
   In the unscarred heaven they leave no wake,
And the eyes forget the tears they have shed,
   The heart forgets its sorrow and ache;
The soul partakes the season's youth,
   And the sulphurous rifts of passion and woe
Lie deep 'neath a silence pure and smooth,
   Like burnt-out craters healed with snow.

Whittier

(*From "A Fable for Critics"*)

There is Whittier, whose swelling and vehement heart
Strains the strait-breasted drab of the Quaker apart,
And reveals the live Man, still supreme and erect,
Underneath the bemummying wrappers of sect;

325

There was ne'er a man born who had more of the swing
Of the true lyric bard and all that kind of thing;
And his failures arise (though he seem not to know it)
From the very same cause that has made him a poet,—
A fervor of mind which knows no separation
'Twixt simple excitement and pure inspiration,
As my Pythoness erst sometimes erred from not knowing
If 'twere I or mere wind through her tripod was blowing;
Let his mind once get head in its favorite direction
And the torrent of verse bursts the dams of reflection,
While, borne with the rush of the metre along,
The poet may chance to go right or go wrong,
Content with the whirl and delirium of song;
Then his grammar's not always correct, nor his rhymes,
And he's prone to repeat his own lyrics sometimes,
Not his best, though, for those are struck off at white-heats
When the heart in his breast like a trip-hammer beats,
And can ne'er be repeated again any more
Than they could have been carefully plotted before:
Like old what's-his-name there at the battle of Hastings
(Who, however, gave more than mere rhythmical bastings),
Our Quaker leads off metaphorical fights
For reform and whatever they call human rights,
Both singing and striking in front of the war,
And hitting his foes with the mallet of Thor;
Anne haec, one exclaims, on beholding his knocks,
Vestis filii tui, O leather-clad Fox?
Can that be thy son, in the battle's mid din,
Preaching brotherly love and then driving it in
To the brain of the tough old Goliath of sin,
With the smoothest of pebbles from Castaly's spring
Impressed on his hard moral sense with a sling?

All honor and praise to the right-hearted bard
Who was true to The Voice when such service was hard,
Who himself was so free he dared sing for the slave
When to look but a protest in silence was brave;
All honor and praise to the women and men
Who spoke out for the dumb and the down-trodden then!
It needs not to name them, already for each
I see History preparing the statue and niche;
They were harsh, but shall *you* be so shocked at hard words
Who have beaten your pruning-hooks up into swords,
Whose rewards and hurrahs men are surer to gain
By the reaping of men and of women than grain?
Why should *you* stand aghast at their fierce wordy war, if
You scalp one another for Bank or for Tariff?
Your calling them cut-throats and knaves all day long
Doesn't prove that the use of hard language is wrong;
While the World's heart beats quicker to think of such men
As signed Tyranny's doom with a bloody steel-pen,
While on Fourth-of-Julys beardless orators fright one
With hints at Harmodius and Aristogeiton,
You need not look shy at your sisters and brothers
Who stab with sharp words for the freedom of others;—
No, a wreath, twine a wreath for the loyal and true
Who, for sake of the many, dared stand with the few,
Not of blood-spattered laurel for enemies braved,
But of broad, peaceful oak-leaves for citizens saved!

Freedom

Men! whose boast it is that ye
Come of fathers brave and free,
If there breathe on earth a slave,

327

Are ye truly free and brave?
If ye do not feel the chain,
When it works a brother's pain,
Are ye not base slaves indeed,
Slaves unworthy to be freed?

Women! who shall one day bear
Sons to breathe New England air.
If ye hear, without a blush,
Deeds to make the roused blood rush
Like red lava through your veins,
For your sisters now in chains,—
Answer! are ye fit to be
Mothers of the brave and free?

Is true Freedom but to break
Fetters for our own dear sake,
And, with leathern hearts, forget
That we owe mankind a debt?
No! true freedom is to share
All the chains our brothers wear,
And, with heart and hand, to be
Earnest to make others free!

They are slaves who fear to speak
For the fallen and the weak;
They are slaves who will not choose
Hatred, scoffing, and abuse,
Rather than in silence shrink,
From the truth they needs must think;
They are slaves who dare not be
In the right with two or three.

HERMAN MELVILLE

(*1819-1891*)

Father Mapple's Hymn

(*From* Moby Dick)

The ribs and terrors in the whale,
    Arched over me a dismal gloom,
While all God's sunlit waves rolled by,
    And left me deepening down to doom.

I saw the opening maw of hell,
    With endless pains and sorrows there;
Which none but they that feel can tell—
    Oh, I was plunging to despair.

In black distress, I called my God,
    When I could scarce believe Him mine,
He bowed his ear to my complaints—
    No more the whale did me confine.

With speed He flew to my relief,
    As on a radiant dolphin borne;
Awful, yet bright as lightning shone
    The face of my Deliverer God.

My song for ever shall record
    That terrible, that joyful hour;
I give the glory to my God,
    His all the mercy and the power.

The Night-March

With banners furled, the clarions mute,
    An army passes in the night;
And beaming spears and helms salute
    The dark with bright.

In silence deep the legions stream,
    With open ranks, in order true;
Over boundless plains they stream and gleam—
    No chief in view!

Afar, in twinkling distance lost
    (So legends tell) he lonely wends
And back through all that shining host
    His mandate sends.

The Maldive Shark

About the Shark, phlegmatical one,
Pale sot of the Maldive sea,
The sleek little pilot-fish, azure and slim,
How alert in attendance be.
From his saw-pit of mouth, from his charnel of maw,
They have nothing of harm to dread,
But liquidly glide on his ghastly flank
Or before his Gorgonian head;
Or lurk in the port of serrated teeth
In white triple tiers of glittering gates,
And there find a haven when peril's abroad,

And asylum in jaws of the Fates!
They are friends; and friendly they guide him to prey,
Yet never partake of the treat—
Eyes and brains to the dotard lethargic and dull,
Pale ravener of horrible meat.

Gold in the Mountain

Gold in the mountain,
And gold in the glen,
And greed in the heart,
Heaven having no part,
And unsatisfied men.

The March into Virginia

(*Ending in the First Manassas. July, 1861*)

Did all the lets and bars appear
   To every just or larger end,
Whence should come the trust and cheer?
   Youth must its ignorant impulse end—
Age finds place in the rear.
   All wars are boyish and are fought by boys,
The champions and enthusiasts of the state;
   Turbid ardours and vain joys
     Not barrenly abate—
   Stimulants to the power mature,
     Preparatives of fate.
Who here forecasteth the event?

331

What heart but spurns at precedent
And warnings of the wise,
Contemned foreclosures of surprise?
The banners play, the bugles call,
The air is blue and prodigal.
　　　No berrying-party, pleasure-wooed,
No picnic party in the May,
Ever went less loth than they
　　　Into that leafy neighborhood.
In Bacchic glee they file toward Fate,
Moloch's uninitiate;
Expectancy, and glad surmise
Of battle's unknown mysteries.
All they feel is this: 'tis glory,
A rapture sharp, though transitory,
Yet lasting in belaurelled story.
So they gaily go to fight,
Chatting left and laughing right.

But some who this blithe mood present,
　　　As on in lightsome files they fare,
Shall die experienced ere three days are spent—
　　　Perish, enlightened by the volleyed glare;
Or shame survive, and, like to adamant,
　　　The throes of Second Manassas share.

From "*The Martyr*"

Good Friday was the day
　　　Of the prodigy and crime,
When they killed him in his pity,

When they killed him in his prime
Of clemency and calm—
   When with yearning he was filled
   To redeem the evil-willed,
And, though conqueror, be kind;
  But they killed him in his kindness,
  In their madness and their blindness,
And they killed him from behind.

   There is sobbing of the strong,
     And a pall upon the land;
  But the People in their weeping
     Bare the iron hand;
  Beware the People weeping
     When they bare the iron hand.

He lieth in his blood—
   The father in his face;
They have killed him, the Forgiver—
   The Avenger takes his place,
The Avenger wisely stern,
     Who in righteousness shall do
     What the heavens call him to,
And the parricides remand;
  For they killed him in his kindness,
  In their madness and their blindness,
And his blood is on their hand.

   There is sobbing of the strong,
     And a pall upon the land;
  But the People in their weeping
     Bare the iron hand;

Beware the People weeping
When they bare the iron hand.

L'Envoi

The Return of the Sire de Nesle: A.D. 16—

My towers at last! These rovings end,
Their thirst is slaked in larger dearth:
The yearning infinite recoils,
   For terrible is earth.

Kaf thrusts his snouted crags through fog:
Araxes swells beyond his span,
And knowledge poured by pilgrimage
   Overflows the banks of man.

But thou, my stay, thy lasting love
One lonely good, let this but be!
Weary to view the wide world's swarm,
   But blest to fold but thee.

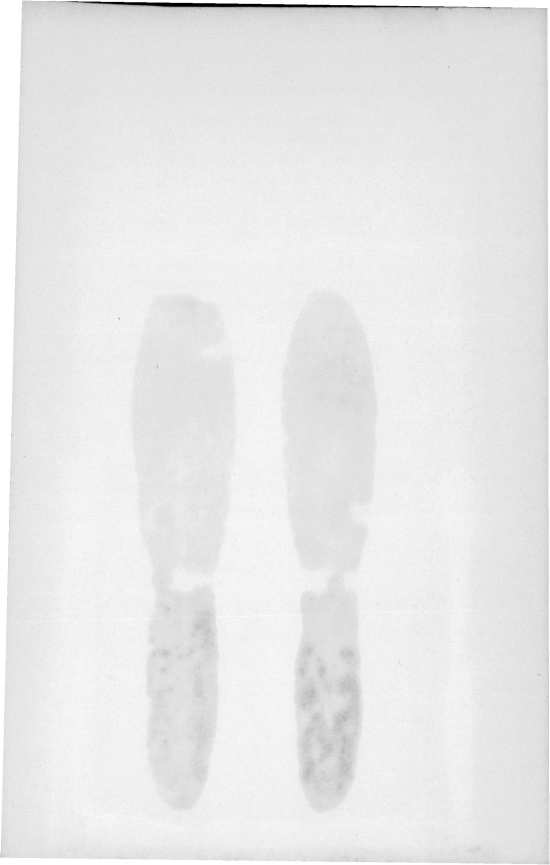